How to Analyze People, Persuasion, and Dark Psychology

(3 Books in 1)

How to recognize the signs of a toxic person manipulating you, and the best defense against it

How to Analyze People, Persuasion, and Dark Psychology

PUBLISHED BY: James W. Williams

© Copyright 2018 - All rights reserved.

The content contained within this book may not be reproduced, duplicated or transmitted without direct written permission from the author or the publisher.

Under no circumstances will any blame or legal responsibility be held against the publisher, or author, for any damages, reparation, or monetary loss due to the information contained within this book. Either directly or indirectly.

Legal Notice:

This book is copyright protected. This book is only for personal use. You cannot amend, distribute, sell, use, quote or paraphrase any part, or the content within this book, without the consent of the author or publisher.

Disclaimer Notice:

Please note the information contained within this document is for educational and entertainment purposes only. All effort has been executed to present accurate, up to date, and reliable, complete information. No warranties of any kind are declared or implied. Readers acknowledge that the author is not engaging in the rendering of legal, financial, medical or professional advice. The content within this book has been derived from various sources. Please consult a licensed professional before attempting any techniques outlined in this book.

By reading this document, the reader agrees that under no circumstances is the author responsible for any losses, direct or indirect, which are incurred as a result of the use of information contained within this document, including, but not limited to, — errors, omissions, or inaccuracies.

James W. Williams

Table of Contents

Your Free Gift 6

Book #1: How to Analyze People 7

Introduction 8

Chapter 1 – Body Language 10

Chapter 2 – Human Psychology 32

Chapter 3 – Subliminal Persuasion 47

Conclusion 57

Book #2: Persuasion 59

Introduction 60

Chapter 1 – Manipulation 62

Chapter 2 – NLP 87

Chapter 3 – Subliminal Persuasion 101

Conclusion 110

Book #3: Dark Psychology 112

Introduction 113

Why I wrote this book 115

PART ONE: FUNDAMENTAL FACTS ABOUT DARK PSYCHOLOGY 119

WHAT IS DARK PSYCHOLOGY? 120

THE EFFECTS AND IMPACT OF DARK PSYCHOLOGY 124

DAY TO DAY EXAMPLES OF DIFFERENT ASPECTS OF DARK PSYCHOLOGY 129

HOW VULNERABLE ARE WE TO DARK PSYCHOLOGY? 134

PART TWO: ANALYZING DARK PSYCHOLOGY **138**

MANIPULATION 139

DECEPTION 143

HYPNOSIS 147

PROBLEMATIC BEHAVIOR 152

REVERSE PSYCHOLOGY 156

PART THREE: KEY AREAS IN OUR LIVES THAT MAKE US VULNERABLE TO DARK PSYCHOLOGY **158**

LOVE AND RELATIONSHIPS 159

BLIND FAITH AND RELIGIOUS BELIEFS 163

SOCIAL CONDITIONING 168

AMBITION AND PERSONAL ASPIRATIONS 173

EMOTIONAL SCARS 178

PART FOUR: RECOGNIZING AND IDENTIFYING YOUR REALITY **183**

ACKNOWLEDGING THE LIES WE TELL OURSELVES 184

IGNORE THE LIS THAT OTHERS TELL US 189
DWELLING ON THE PAST 194
BLIND OPTIMISM 199
THE VICIOUS CYCLE 204
PART FIVE: HOW TO BREAK FREE **209**
ACCEPT THAT YOU HAVE A PROBLEM 210
ACT QUICKLY 214
GET HELP FAST 218
DON'T COVER UP 222
FORGIVE YOURSELF 226
TRUST YOUR INSTINCTS 230
EMPLOY THE BEST PRACTICES IN ALL YOUR DEALINGS .. 234
CONCLUSION 237

Thank you 239

How to Analyze People, Persuasion, and Dark Psychology

Your Free Gift

As a way of saying thanks for your purchase, I wanted to offer you a free bonus E-book called **Bulletproof Confidence Checklist** exclusive to the readers of this book.

To get instant access just go to:

https://theartofmastery.com/confidence/

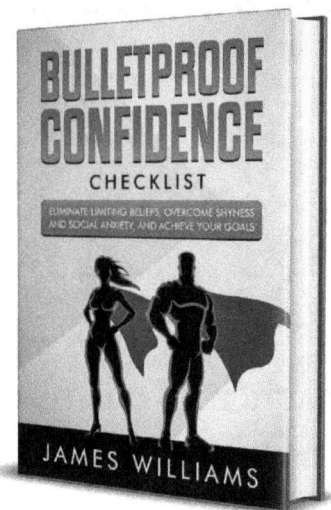

Inside the book, you will discover:

- What is shyness & social anxiety, and the psychology behind it
- Simple yet powerful strategies for overcoming social anxiety
- Breakdown of the traits of what makes a confident person
- Traits you must DESTROY if you want to become confident
- Easy techniques you can implement TODAY to keep the conversation flowing
- Confidence checklist to ensure you're on the right path of self-development

James W. Williams

How to Analyze People

Dark Psychology

Dark Secrets to Analyze and Influence Anyone Using Body Language, Human Psychology, Subliminal Persuasion and NLP

Introduction

In my book *Persuasion,* the different ways that we have been persuaded were touched on. Many of us might have gone a long time in our lives without even realizing that we had been persuaded and manipulated so often. The damages of this manipulation can last forever, and it can be hard to recover. Once you become aware of how others might be subliminally persuading you, you can better protect yourself from these tactics in the future to maintain your independence and stay out of others' influence.

It's important to remember that by understanding these concepts you're better equipped to identify and defend against them, and your new knowledge shouldn't be about how you can use those same tactics to manipulate other people. There is a difference between evil manipulation and trying to convince someone of something else. You don't want to trick someone into doing things for you when they won't get any benefit at all. You only want to use these tactics when you need to persuade someone for something and you can't blatantly ask them for help. There are people that are harder to convince than others, so you might need to use some strategies of persuasion.

Who might you need to persuade? You never want to take advantage of someone that already doesn't have much to give. Those you should be trying to persuade are people that hold power. You might want to learn how to convince your boss to get a raise. Maybe you want to try to get your girlfriend to move in with you. Perhaps you have to ask your parents for a loan. You don't want to "punch down," but instead, "reach up."

This book will start with how you can analyze other people. Once you have a better understanding of how to analyze those around you both physically and psychologically, you'll be able to persuade them better towards your favor.

Chapter 1 – Body Language

One of the easiest ways to analyze other people is to look at their body language. How a person holds themselves, moves, and even speaks can tell you a lot about them. Everyone has plenty of variation between their mannerisms, and there's no exact way to tell what makes up a person. There are still many similar indications among groups of people that can give you a deep insight into how someone functions.

It's not easy because it starts with becoming aware of your own body language. In order to understand and attempt to overcome the enigma that is body language, you have to be hyper aware. In book one, we took you through the process of becoming aware of your thoughts and where they might come from. Now it's time to work on becoming aware of your body. In order to learn what makes a person different from others based on their body language, you have to first look at yourself and analyze how you hold your body.

Some people might be more aware of their movements than they are their thoughts. Women are likely going to be more aware of their bodies and the space they take up, mostly because of the patriarchal society we grew up in. Everyone still might find difficulty in confronting the way they hold their body. You can lose focus while trying to maintain awareness, becoming too insecure with your own body and movements.

This first chapter will go into the basics of body language while also laying a basis for how you can analyze others. Once you get to know the body movements better of another person, you can also understand what makes them unique. The more you know about a person, the better you can conclude the best strategy for persuasion.

Cultural Differences

Every person is different, and sometimes, how one person holds their body has a different meaning than someone who stands the same way. There are plenty of ways that a person's body language differs, so it's important to remember that not everything about a certain body movement is 100% true for every person. This is especially important to remember when talking to people with different cultural backgrounds.

There are some cultures that practice modesty, so touching might be completely off limits. Other cultures might be more open to expressing their feelings through their bodies, so culture is important to remember when thinking about how a person might use their body.

Studying Others' Movements

Once you become more aware of body movements and what they might represent, you can start studying them when interacting with different people. Everyone you come in contact with uses their body to represent different things. Some people are closed off, and others might be more open. These are some small differences you could tell just by observing someone's body language.

When studying other people and yourself, it's important to try and act naturally as well. It can be easy to become hyper-aware of your movements but know that you don't have to hold your body a certain way. Not everyone is as aware of body movements as others might be, so at the end of the day, don't look into your own movements too much.

Still, once you start studying others' body movements, you'll start to realize how much you can get to know them. Certain things might all start to make sense after meeting a variety of individuals. You might notice that one of your friends is rather pretentious in the way they hold themselves or talk. Other friends might show how insecure they are with themselves, even though you thought they had been incredibly confident since you'd known them.

Knowing a person's body language and having insight as to why they might move a certain way can allow you to understand them at their core better. This gives you better leverage when it comes to persuading them. You might want to match the confidence of your boss when striking up a deal for a raise. Perhaps you noticed you need to be more relaxed around certain friends that seem to be shy or nervous. Becoming aware of your body language can be scary at first, but eventually, you'll be comfortable with the way you move.

To start practicing being comfortable with your own body, try hanging out in front of a mirror. When you're eating dinner, watching TV, or even lounging in bed, set up a mirror so you can see how you hold yourself. Once you get an outsider's perspective on how you move, you'll be able to see how others move as well.

Eye Contact

Eye contact is one of the biggest clues you can use to determine how someone truly is. It's important to become aware of your own use of eye contact as well, because it gives others clues about your personality and true nature. Maintaining eye contact is important to let a person know that you're interested in what they're saying and that they have your full attention.

It can also be overused, however, and let people know that you're trying too hard to convince them that you're listening. Too much eye contact can sometimes intimidate others as well, so if you notice that a person is getting nervous because of the amount of eye contact you're having with them, change it up every now and then.

Pupil dilation can be a direct indication that a person is interested in what you're saying. Studies have proven that when a person's pupils begin dilating whom you're making eye contact with, they are more interested in what you have to say. They are listening to you with their utmost attention, and they're thinking deeply about what you're saying. You know when a person's pupils are dilated while talking to you that they are legitimately interested in the conversation.

Shifty eyes will indicate the opposite. Someone who is looking at your eyes back and forth is probably trying to convince you that they are listening. They are aware that they need to try and make eye contact, but they are completely zoned out with what you are saying. Those with shifty eyes might also be lying to you or trying to deceit you in some way. They might be having difficulty maintaining eye contact with you because they know they are being deceitful.

Mouth Movements

What someone does with their mouth is very crucial in understanding their personality as well. Someone with tight or pursed lips might be trying to concentrate, or they also might be trying hard to hide a sour face. You can analyze a person's smile as well. If the corners of their eyes aren't creased, they might be forcing a smile with you.

Someone that's faking a smile isn't necessarily evil, they might just be thinking of something else, too distracted to give their full attention to what you're saying. Sometimes, smiles are also reactions to uncomfortable situations.

When monkeys smile, it's not because they are happy, but mostly because they are showing their teeth as a way of threatening those around them. When they feel scared and nervous, they'll open their mouths wide, showing that they have teeth they could use to hurt. The same goes for dogs. They only show their teeth when they are feeling threatened. For humans, this can be true sometimes as well, but on a subconscious level.

Nervous laughing and smiling are just a way for a person to alleviate their tension. You can tell someone is genuinely smiling when they have creases in the corners of their eyes.

A person that is continually covering their mouth also is usually nervous. They might bite their lip, finger, or put a fist over their mouth. Knowing when a person is uncomfortable or nervous can sometimes be helpful when trying to persuade them. We'll discuss how and when to use this knowledge to persuade others in the next two chapters.

Nodding

How a person turns and tilts their head can be a subtle movement. Most of the time, others aren't as aware when they are moving their head around. The neck and head movements of the person you're talking to can give you great insight into what they might be thinking on a deeper level.

Someone that nods their head rather quickly while listening to you might just be anxious, trying to move the conversation along as quick as possible. They're attempting to set a pace for you so that you speak faster. They want to let you know they hear you, but you're not speaking fast enough. If someone is doing this to you, try to speed up your words in order to hold their attention.

Someone who tilts their head to the side might have a legitimate interest in what you're saying. They are attempting to turn an ear towards you, so they can hear you better, whether they're aware of their movements or not. They also are indicating to you that they hear you and they want you to keep talking. It's a way for them to get closer to you in the conversation without having to make any interjections or interruptions.

If someone is nodding too artificially, they might just be attempting to convince you that they are interested in what you are saying. They could be aware that they should be paying attention, but they might have lost interest. In an attempt to keep up, they pretend to nod their head. They also might not understand what you're saying, so they nod to make you think they're keeping up. If you notice others around you are artificially nodding their head, it'd be worth it to either change the subject to regain attention or explain yourself better as they might just be confused.

Mimicking someone's head movements can be very helpful in using persuasion. A gentle tilt of the head while listening to them can show that you are comprehending what they're saying. It can also show that you're empathetic to them, especially if they seem to be talking about something that is hard for them.

Hands and Arms

How someone uses their hands and arms is another way that body language can be interpreted to get a better understanding of the people you're interacting with. Our hands represent so much about ourselves. They're a way of expressing out stories, putting different emphasis on various parts. If someone's telling a story, they're going to use hand gestures to keep people interested. Think of someone engaged in a conversation as someone that's directing an orchestra. They'll lift their hands to keep up a rhythm and pace for those listening around.

Someone's hands and arms can also express how open or closed off they are. They can be like the doorway into someone's body. If they're crossed tightly in front of someone's chest, that person might be a little more closed off, not wanting to engage too much in conversation. Having their arms crossed doesn't always mean that someone is necessarily closed off. They might also just be wanting to rest their arms, so if they're loosely hanging in front of their chest, they're likely just casually listening to you.

Someone that has their arms outstretched, maybe over their head, will likely be very open and possibly even trying to exert power over a situation. Someone with their hands on their hips might also be trying to assert their power.

Signals

Everyone has different body language ques that they use as signals. Between cultures, genders, and ages, different movements someone makes with their bodies can be conscious or subconscious signals that they're giving to the people around them. Signals let other people know bits of information without having to say anything at all.

Someone with their arms crossed, eyes fading on a couch at a party is giving the signal that they're likely ready to head home for the night. Someone else on that couch could be sitting on the edge of their seat, laughing loudly, signaling they're not going to be heading to bed anytime soon.

Signals help the people around the signaler know things that they might not easily be able to express with their bodies. Some are very good at picking up on other people's signals, and some people struggle to understand those around them.

When it comes to trying to persuade someone, there are some crucial signals that a person will need to be able to properly lead a conversation.

Starting a Conversation

Next time you're sitting quietly in a room with another

person, wait until they start the conversation to speak. This will allow you to study how they might start a conversation. Most people will give some sort of signal with their body that they are about to begin speaking. They might clear their throat, turn their head, adjust their shirt, or shift in their seat. There is usually something, no matter how small it might be, that a person does right before they start a conversation.

When it comes to your turn to start a conversation, notice what you do before you begin speaking. Don't start with an "um," or "uh." That lets the other person know right away that you're not very sure about what you're going to say. Try starting a conversation without doing anything. See if you can just start speaking without clearing your throat, moving your head, or doing anything else. Study how the other person reacts. They might be surprised or thrown off guard that one of you had started speaking.

Starting a conversation, especially one that is meant to persuade another person, is important for laying the groundwork for your argument. No one is going to want to give their full attention to someone that is struggling to start. If you're nervous and jumping over your words right off the bat, it's going to be much harder to keep up.

Leading the Conversation

Once the conversation has started, it can be tricky to maintain the right amount of back and forth. You don't want to be too pushy, but you also don't want to let them talk too much, not allowing you anytime to state your points. If you feel as though the other person isn't letting you talk enough, there are obvious phrases you can use to speak your mind. You might try saying something like, "can I just say...," "could I speak for a minute?" or "I'm listening but can I say something really quick?"

These can be hard to say in some situations, and some people might even perceive you as being rude if you make a large interjection. What your best option might be is to use your body to redirect focus. Put your hands on your hips or tilt your head to let the other person know that you have something to say. Try leaning in to let them know that you want to take over as the leader of your current conversation.

Leading the conversation can be tricky, because no one wants to listen to someone that is interrupting them. It's still important that you get your turn to speak as well. There are ways you can practice leading conversations so that when it comes time to have an important persuasion, you can properly lead. Next time you want to say something, don't. Instead let the other person continue speaking and interject later. Sometimes we get so anxious to say our part we distract from the true conversation, invalidating any argument we have to the person that we interrupted.

An alternative way to practice leading the conversation is to speak up the next time you want to say something. If you have something to say but you would rather just keep quiet, force yourself to say what you want. These two methods of practice will give you two alternate perspectives on leading a conversation that you might not get otherwise.

How Your Body Language Affects You

Believe it or not, how you use your body can directly affect how you function as well. There are ways that you can use to improve how you think, and the capacity of your memory just by the way that you use your hands and arms. Not only are there physical differences in terms of how you use your body, but you will also be affected by the way others perceive you.

If you're constantly closed off, always crossing your arms, there are probably a lot of people that might not open up or talk to you because they assume you have no interest in conversation. If you're always very open with your body, exerting confidence and holding yourself high, others might end up being intimidated by you. You might not have any intention of closing others off or being intimidating, but your body can show that in ways that your mouth doesn't.

It can be tricky to become self-aware of your body movements, but once you do, you can really alter what someone thinks of you. There are some people that might have a strong conscious mind, but perhaps they hate their body. They then might close others off by trying to hide their bodies, making others think that they're judgmental. Sometimes, a person is just trying to cover up their body and not themselves. You would be surprised at how much confidence you can feel just by changing up the way you hold your body. People can still see what you look like even if you keep your arms crossed. You might think you're altering other's perceptions of you, but really, you're just remaining closed off.

There are other ways that your own body language can

actually mentally affect you.

Open Your Mind

Someone that starts opening their arms when they talk will begin to let others know that they are much more open-minded. If you stand with arms open, or just hanging relaxed by your side, you let the people around you know that you are confident and willing to talk with them about different things.

While having open arms is a signal for others, it's also a signal for your brain. Studies show that by standing with open arms verses crossed ones, you can actually signal your brain to be more open. You'll start to think of new ideas that you wouldn't if you kept your arms crossed. The same goes for the rest of your body. The more open you are with your movements, the more you allow your brain to have different ideas.

Improve Your Memory

Those that talk with their hands also tend to have a better memory than those that don't. Using your hands can put physical reminders in your brain for ideas and thoughts that you might be discussing. If you mimic numbers or shapes when you're talking about different ideas, especially in a business setting, not only will you remember what you're discussing better, but those around you will find your story more memorable as well.

Using your hands to talk while telling a story will also help you remember the things that you went through. You're encouraging your brain to continue thinking, and keeping your arms open, just as we mentioned in the last section, will open up your brain to new thoughts and feelings you might not have had should you have spoken with your arms crossed and closed off.

Verbal Cues

While there are many things that a person can say with their body, there are many more things that they can say with their mouth. There's a seemingly limitless amount of languages out there, as each specific language has many subparts. Think of how many different accents there might be in just New York City. As we continue to develop and blend different cultures and languages, only more will develop. It's hard enough to keep up with what we already know, but there are ways to still pick up on others' meaning without having to memorize every word in the dictionary.

Just because a person says a certain word doesn't indicate that they're actually meaning what they say. How many times have you said you were "fine," when really, you wanted to explode with thoughts? We say what we don't mean all the time because it isn't always easy to put words to our thoughts and feelings. Many people take their frustration or sadness out on other people when they don't actually mean anything that they're saying.

Knowing why people say the things they do can be one of the trickiest codes to try and crack. You don't always have to know exactly what a person means in order to understand what they're trying to say. You can pick up on what a person's intention is by listening to how they talk and mixing that with their body language. It's important to read someone's mood so you don't say the wrong thing or anything that could potentially change the direction of the conversation.

Next time you find something on TV that's in a different language than any you can speak, try watching without subtitles. You'll be surprised to see that you actually understand part of the storyline. Don't look at what they're saying, but how they're saying it. Is there pain in their eyes? Do they look happy or sad? Sometimes if you can't understand what a person is saying, maybe because the room is loud or they're speaking softly, try looking into their eyes. You might get a better sense of what they're saying than if you just watch the words their mouth is attempting to put together.

There are certain specific cues that someone can give when they're trying to direct a conversation. When you're trying to persuade someone, you might want to try and use different keywords to help you in leading the conversation. Some people get too hung up on the actual words someone is saying when they should just be trying to listen to the message they're getting across.

It can seem difficult to try to crack what someone else means, but it can be done. Think about your pets. You can tell if your dog is sad, sleepy, hungry, or in a playful mood, but you don't have actual conversations with them. Sometimes you can analyze what a person is saying best by figuring out the noises they're making rather than dissecting every word that they say.

Emphasis Cues

When trying to persuade someone, you're going to want to have a pretty good argument already prepared in order to build your case. You might want to include some emphasis cues when you're speaking. It can be hard to incorporate these phrases naturally, but it's good to practice so you can become a better persuader.

"This is important," "you need to know," "let me explain," are all phrases that grab the attention of the person that you're speaking too. You might start to notice others' emphasis cues better after reading this section as well. You should be listening, and using in your own speech, phrases that seem to put emphasis on an important part of a conversation.

Sometimes, these emphasis cues aren't even actual phrases. They might just be verbal indications that something is important, such as someone raising their voice when talking about an important part of their argument. They also might repeat the word several times or stop for a pause in order for the listener to take in what they just said. Emphasis cues are important to understand in order to get a better grasp of what might be important to an individual. If you listen to what they're putting emphasis on, you'll be able to also formulate your thoughts and arguments around the things that are important to them.

Organizational Cues

"First, second, third," "to summarize," "the topic is," are all phrases that could be considered organizational cues. These cues help a person indicate that they are trying to organize their thoughts, again, maybe putting emphasis on the things that are the most important.

Organizational cues are important for you to use in your arguments in persuasions in order to get people on your side. You want them to know that you're listening to what they have to say, and that they should be listening to you. You're trying to formulate a plan based on both your thoughts and opinions, and not just the words of one specific individual.

Organizational cues allow the speaker to put emphasis on what's important while also maintaining a clear thought and direct focus. Organizational cues might not be phrases either. It could just be someone clearing their throat, redirecting the conversation back to a previous topic, or stopping in order for everyone to collect their thoughts.

Watch Your Pitch

Pitch is an important key when trying to direct one's conversation in their favor. Pitch is the level of your voice, and the overall sound quality. Someone with a deep pitch might have a more soothing tone, while someone with a high-pitched voice might make their listeners more alert. Not everyone can help the natural pitch of their voice. There are some people that have extremely low voices that are hard to hear, and some people just have naturally shrill voices that seem as though they bother everyone around them!

While your natural pitch can't always be controlled, you can at least help direct that pitch towards a more productive tone in order to keep your listeners engaged with what you have to say. Many of us let our pitch become too high and whiny when we are in professional settings, trying to keep our dictation sharp. If you feel like your voice is becoming high and shrill, don't be afraid to stop, clear your throat, and start again. The people around you will likely be grateful that you're adjusting your tone for their listening pleasure.

Be careful not to let the end of your voice go up when speaking. Many people, especially when talking on a phone, tend to let the end of their words go up like they're asking a question. This kind of speaking is also common among those that might be giving a speech. They'll say a phrase very clearly with dictation, but they'll also end the sentence in a high pitched way as if they're asking a question. This is something that should be avoided in order to keep the attention of your listeners.

It's important to find your optimal pitch. Some people have very soft voices that can be hard to hear. If this is the case, it's important to practice speaking up when it's necessary. Someone that tends to speak loudly should try talking low as often as possible to help balance their pitch out. The greatest way to practice is alone, and if you record what you're saying. You don't want to deeply analyze the way you speak too much, but practicing always helps, especially for those that find difficulty in speaking their voice.

It's also important to have a confident pitch to let others know they should listen to you. Someone that's always talking timidly or like they're asking a question will let the others around them know that what they have to say isn't interesting. If you're so unsure of what you're saying, why should someone else listen to you? The best way to ensure others are paying attention is to make sure that you speak with confidence.

Listen to Others

Talking about yourself can elicit the same good feelings that money and food cause. People like talking about themselves more than they enjoy listening to other people talk about themselves for the most part. While it can seem selfish, it's true that most people would prefer to talk about themselves. This means that when conversing with other people, you should avoid talking about yourself too much.

You don't want to make the conversation completely about other people, but no one will pay attention if the only thing you talk about is yourself. Giving advice can also be helpful, but people generally don't engage as often with those that offer too much advice, especially when it isn't asked for.

Listening to other people can actually be challenging for some. They might find it difficult to not let their mind wander, especially if the other person is talking too much about themselves. Some people will find that they're usually forming their next thought while the other person is talking instead of actually listening to them. If you find your mind wandering when someone else is talking, redirect your thoughts back to their words. Don't just listen to what they're saying. Watch how they're saying it. Listen to their voice and look into their eyes. People will notice whether or not you're listening to them. Even if they aren't skilled in body language, they will still be able to at least sense that you might not be fully engaged as well.

Don't just put an emphasis on listening to others. Make the conversation about them as well. Ask questions about the person, attempting to get to know them better. You'll find that people usually like to answer questions about themselves. This is often a technique you'll see in many salespeople. They'll ask where you got your shirt, or if you've had a good day. This is to get the person thinking about themselves, and they'll usually end up opening up a bit more to the salesperson as well.

People don't like to be corrected. While it can be hard to avoid sometimes, most people don't want to be interrupted to be told that they were wrong. Most people will respect you much more if you just let them talk rather than trying to prove them wrong. This is very important to remember, especially when trying to persuade and analyze others.

Talk about "we," not "you." If you're trying to make suggestions, maybe to a spouse or friend about an improvement in their lifestyle, use "we" instead. Don't say, "you should try waking up earlier on the weekends," say, "we should get up early on Sunday and go on a walk together!" People will respond much better to suggestions if you include yourself.

Apologizing

It can be hard to apologize, especially for those with high levels of pride, but it's important in gaining the respect of the people around you. If you apologize for being late rather than giving every explanation you can, most will respond much better to this than if you were to try to make yourself look better with excuses.

They also like to see humility, and that you maybe aren't afraid to express yourself. If you can open up with someone and just say, "I'm sorry I didn't respond to your text, I was just having a really bad day," they'll usually be very forgiving rather than if you would've just blown them off.

However, don't apologize too much. It can lead others to not trust you. Sometimes we have the urge to apologize for things that were out of our control in an attempt to make ourselves look better. We'll say, "I'm sorry the movie was so bad!" after going out for a movie night, even though we had no control over the production. This is nice every once in a while, and certainly shows humility and vulnerability to those around you. But too much of it can also make you seem untrustworthy to others.

If you have to apologize after every little thing you say, why should anyone listen to you in the first place? Next time you feel the urge to apologize for something that was out of your control, try saying thank you instead. After having a long conversation with a friend, don't say, "Sorry you had to listen to me rant!" Instead, try something like, "Thank you for being such a great listener. I'm glad to have a friend like you!" People will generally respond much more positively to a thankful person than someone that always invalidates themselves. You'll find that you start to treat yourself much better if you stick to this method of apology as well.

The Power of Your Body

Our bodies have so much power, and not just with how much we're able to lift or carry. Physical strength is important, but even the weakest of people have the ability to control a room with their body movements alone. At this point in the book, you should have a basic understanding of what a person's body language might mean.

We can't get into every specific detail of what someone's physical actions might be trying to convey, but the framework for how to analyze those movements is there. Once you understand how someone else might be using their body to persuade others, you can start to work on your own skills of persuasion.

There are many ways that someone can use their body to convince others to do what they want, but it won't always work on everyone. Some people respond to sexual persuasion while others are repulsed by the thought. Some people respond to a physical threat from those that seem stronger than them, but others might be ready for the fight.

There are plenty of ways that you can use your body to persuade others without being sexual or physically intimidating. Keeping your body open and visible is crucial in letting others know they can trust you. Try making sure to remove physical barriers that might keep you separated from the person you're talking to. Step around a chair or table that's blocking you from making a full connection with the person you're trying to talk to.

This also shows that you're confident and interested in speaking your mind while hearing what the other person has to say as well. When analyzing other people's movements, you can also figure out what things you can do yourself to be more confident. Study certain celebrities and see how they hold themselves in various scenarios. Everyone has their own movements, but mimicking others can still help you find your own footing when it comes to having a persuasive demeanor overall.

Smiling is Important

Our smiles are one of the most powerful tools we've been given. You can turn any situation from bad to good just by turning up the corners of your mouth. Some people feel as though if they don't have straight teeth or smiles that are bright white, they aren't worth anything. Even those that don't have all their teeth can have much more beautiful smiles than someone that's spent thousands on dental work.

A smile isn't just about what teeth you're showing. It's a way to engage another person. Studies have proven that most people will smile if someone else smiles at them first. If they do smile, they'll end up having a better mood overall. It can seem weird, but simply smiling can lift someone's spirits. Next time you are feeling particularly down, smile. It sounds so silly, but it might work. Smile over and over again, and even though it might not turn your mood around, it will certainly help to at least temporarily lift your spirits.

Chapter 2 – Human Psychology

You don't have to be a psychology expert to have a basic understanding of how the human brain works. Once you get to know how our brains operate, you can begin to analyze people much more easily. You'll start to realize that those around might act a certain way because of the way they were raised and the things that they were taught. Once you have a basic understanding of human psychology, you'll start to put together the pieces of what makes the people around you the unique individuals they are. You'll realize a lot more makes sense about why a person does the things they do if you can look into their psychology.

Even those incredibly skilled in human psychology make mistakes every now and then. There is still so little known about the human brain that of course, not everyone is going to be right all the time. The brain is the most complex organ in the body of any animal, not just humans. It can be hard to understand it and figure out what secrets lie inside that make a person tick. You can still attempt to get to know the inner workings of a person's brain, and even though you won't have all the answers, you'll start to understand them a little better.

There is little known about the human brain, and what is known has been discovered by the brain itself! Isn't it strange to think that everything we know about the brain was taught to us by our own brains? This complex organ will never fully make sense to anyone, but that's part of the fun of trying to discover someone.

It's important to not use someone's own psyche against them. The intention should never be to persuade people to do something in which only you gain. Some people have more sensitive brains that are more susceptible to influence. While some people choose to remain ignorant, others legitimately don't have what it takes to grasp that they might be getting taken advantage of. You should never knowingly take advantage of another person that can't understand what's going on.

Some people require tactful approach, mostly because they aren't ready to confront their own issues. Not everyone has even a basic understanding of their brain or why it does and thinks the things it does. Some people are afraid of their own minds, so they aren't as willing to confront themselves and their emotions as other people might be. It's important to remain patient with those that might not be as self-aware as you.

Creating Vulnerability

Others respond well when one presents themselves as vulnerable. Humans connect on a societal, human, and animalistic levels. In all three of those categories, vulnerability is sought in order to make a connection. No one wants to feel as though they're talking to a refrigerator. Vulnerability is important in letting the other person know that you are human as well.

It's comforting to know there is another person that's relatable. We all have our flaws, conscious mistakes, and days when we're just lazy. Some of us have days when it can be difficult to even get out of bed. If you can show part of this side to another human, they'll be more likely to connect with you. Many of us desire to be that perfect person that's seemingly flawless. We look at those Instagram celebrities, see their perfect skin and hair, and deep down, wish that we could be like them. Most people don't realize that they wouldn't want to be friends with this person, however. There needs to be a balance when making deeper connections, so presenting yourself as too unattainable, too perfect, will only drive others away in the end.

Vulnerability is dangerous when it becomes codependency. Of course, it's good to show others that you're a real human with thoughts and feelings. However, sometimes, people become too dependent on others when trying to make a connection with them, and they end up dabbling in the dangerous world of codependency. When you get rid of your own thoughts and feelings and start to take on the opinions of others around you too much, there's a chance you might have some codependent tendencies.

There are ways that a person can present themselves as vulnerable, and they'll find that people respond well to this. Sharing too much is something that can make many people uncomfortable. You don't have to tell everyone your darkest secrets to make them think that you have a vulnerable side. There are other ways to prove to those around you that you are a relatable person that they can make a connection with.

Ask for Help

Asking for help is a way to present vulnerability. You're letting the other person know that not only do you need them, but you're choosing to ask them for help. You're going out of your way to let them know that they have what it takes to solve your problem. You're giving another person responsibility over yourself, and that can make them feel very powerful.

It seems as though it would be counterproductive. Why would you want to show yourself as helpless to another person? The key is to not ask for too much help. You don't want to put someone else in an uncomfortable scenario where they have to do a great favor for you. Just asking for little things, to borrow something, to join you while you shop, or to house sit for a weekend, these small things can help connect you to someone you might not otherwise be able to relate to.

By creating an interaction between you and the other person, you can connect with them on a human level. You're putting more value into your relationship than if you were to keep things on a conversational level. You'll see this a lot with teachers and those that care for children. They ask the kids to do something so the children can feel important, like they have meaning. They can then connect to the adults with these small tasks. The same thinking can be carried into adulthood.

Ask for More

One way to ensure that you'll be able to persuade someone to help is by asking for more than you need in order to ensure that you'll at least get half. If you need to borrow someone's truck to help you move, ask if they can help you pack, unpack, and unload your belongings. This is a lot to ask of a person, so there's a chance they'll say no. If they do, then you could just ask to borrow their truck, the main reason you asked for help in the first place. They'll be much more likely to say yes, because they feel bad about turning down your first request.

This is a good technique that you can use in certain business negotiations. When putting an offer on a house, you're not going to offer what you actually want to pay. You'll go lower to give the other person a chance to counter back. This same kind of thinking can be applied to different interactions and moments of persuasion with other people, both on a business and personal level.

You still have to be reasonable with your requests. You can't expect to use this method to change a person. If you want more emotionally from a person, you won't be able to ask for twice as much as what you need, as everyone has their own pace. This method of persuasion isn't applicable in every scenario, but it can certainly help you in many different situations.

Making Connections

Making connections is an important part of analyzing and persuading another person. No one wants to do favors for someone they have no relationship with. No one will be able to have a genuinely happy relationship with a person that they don't feel anything for. Some people are harder to make connections with. They might have spent a good portion of their lives closed off, not wanting to meet new people. This is often because they've been hurt so often that they don't want to let themselves feel pain again. They've become an independent person that's relied on themselves and only their self for so long to provide happiness. While these people might be the most challenging to connect with, it's still possible. You have to present yourself as more vulnerable in order to let them know that you don't want to hurt them.

You can't make yourself too needy, as independent people don't like those that seem to be too reliant on other people. It's not easy to find that balance, but it is possible.

It can be hard for individuals to figure out how to even make connections. They might feel like they don't fit in, and no one understands them. Many people would be surprised to find out that there are actually many others like them that feel the same way. Even those that seemingly fit in and get along with everyone will find that they still have their moments of loneliness.

Sometimes, being a human can be incredibly lonely. You feel empty inside with your own thoughts sometimes, wondering if you can even trust and rely on yourself, let alone the people around you. This feeling of loneliness might never go away but connecting with other people can help alleviate those feelings. Letting other people know that they're not alone can also help you feel connected to others as well. There are plenty of ways to get a deeper connection with those you already know and love, but when it comes to meeting new people, there are a few methods you can use to make a connection.

Use their Name

People enjoy when you use their name. It reminds them that you're connecting to them. Bosses that can call out their employees by name are much more likely to be respected. No matter how big a company might be or how many employees there are, it's always a good idea to make sure you know as many people's names as possible. The same should be said for those that are around often. Get to know the name of your mailman, or the person that makes your coffee at Starbucks every morning.

Some people think reading the nametags of workers can be a way to connect with them, but it's always better to wait for someone to introduce themselves, or to ask them their name. Your server might have a nametag on, but instead of just calling them out, introduce yourself. People feel much more comfortable if you call them by their name, if they know your name as well.

When talking to people and having serious conversations with them, it's important to still use someone's name as well. It brings them back into the conversation and lets them know you're talking specifically about the two of you, not just generally. Many people might even realize they don't call their own spouse by their name because they've spent so much time talking *at* them and not *to* them.

Mirroring Behavior

Once you can start picking up on someone's body language, you can start to understand how to mimic their behavior. Someone that seems very confident, always standing with their arms above their heads or with them pointed out on their sides might be harder to match, but it's still important to try and mimic this behavior. Matching confidence is crucial, especially in a deal where you're trying to persuade the other person.

You don't want to do this to be manipulative, but rather, to make them feel comfortable. Some people might notice that a person is feeling particularly uncomfortable, so they might take advantage of this and exert their confidence and power over the other person. This should never be done, as you're closing off the opportunity for them to open up to you.

If you notice someone is uncomfortable and closed off, reduce your confidence level to match. It lets them know that they can trust you and depend on you. If someone is picking at their fingers and rapidly tapping their feet out of anxiety, you don't have to do the same. Just make sure that you're at their level or lower, whether that means you have to sit or stand. Then keep your arms relaxed, maybe tilting your head to let them know that you're listening and ready to hear what they have to say. You don't want to make anyone feel more uncomfortable than they already are.

Flattery gets you everywhere

Sometimes, sucking up to someone can really work. You don't want to be inauthentic or too over the top with what compliments you're giving to another person, but it's still important to remember just how much a little extra love can go. There's a chance you're already thinking the things you want to say anyway, so why not tell them how you feel, as long as it's positive.

Flattery doesn't just have to be telling someone how gorgeous or smart they are. It can be as simple as picking up their favorite snack when you're at the store or remembering to ask how their vacation went if you know they went away for the weekend. Some people might see these things as "kissing ass," or "brown nosing," but trying to make a positive connection should be part of our everyday life.

Even if someone sees what you're doing, they're still appreciative of your conscious effort to make a connection. It can be pretty obvious in some instances that a person is trying to flatter you, especially if they're normally closed off or seemingly careless. While some people can be bothered by this, most will still appreciate the effort you're putting into trying to make a connection with them.

The Power of Words

You, because, free, instantly, and new, these are the most powerful words in the English language. "You," is an important word, because people love hearing about themselves. Listen to a 1-3-year-old talk next time you're around them. "Me," and "mine," are likely going to be a huge part of their vocabulary. It might even be the first word most people learn!

"Because," is an important word, because many people are looking for an explanation. In a word with so many curiosities and possibilities, we can feel overwhelmed with how little we know. Humans are obsessed with labels, and most people like to know the reason behind something. When they hear the word "because," their brain kicks on and becomes more alert, waiting for the explanation they're so desperately seeking.

"Free" is a popular word, for many reasons in our society. On one hand, it means free stuff! People will spend three hundred dollars on something they don't need if it means they get one small FREE gift to go along with that. You can really hypnotize someone by using the word "free."

"Free," is also an important word because so many people desire freedom and independence in their lives. Even the most codependent people like to hear the word "free," even if it's just them getting an illusion of what freedom might mean.

"Instantly," is a great word because so many people are obsessed with time. We all have to face the dark truth: we're going to die one day. Even those that are in their 20s still have to know that their days are numbered. We try to fight change as much as possible, but time is unbeatable, so when we can get more of it, we're hooked, someone promising something instant is going to be popular.

"New," is the last of the five most popular words. As humans, our brains are wired to constantly look for new growth. Some people might be afraid of change, but we still look for new things. "New," represents growth and life at the same time. Some people might want to wear the same shirt they've had for years versus a brand new one. Still, if offered a new or an old sandwich, they're going to go for the new one.

These five words are very important to include in everyone's vocabulary, whether you're trying to persuade someone or not.

What you do with your body is important, but the words that you decide to share are crucial as well. It's important to remember not only with what you're saying, but with what others are speaking as well. Not everything that is said is exactly what is meant.

Psychological Theories

Most of us learned in early elementary school what a scientific theory was. It usually involved the idea of someone who then tests that theory to see if what they believed is right. A psychological theory is similar, in that a psychiatrist or psychologist thought of something they saw among their patients, decided to test their theory, and then got differing results. There are numerous psychological theories that are important, and the more you know, the better you'll be able to analyze someone else.

There is a lot to know about different psychology aspects in order to understand all of the psychological theories the world of science has to offer. Not everyone has to be a therapist or psychiatrist to understand what some different psychological theories might be.

You should try coming up with your own as well. Maybe you noticed a behavior among a group of people that you interact with. What is the root cause for them reacting this way? How might they react differently to a certain stimulus versus another group of people? Everyone is different, so not every theory is going to apply. It's still very interesting to see how often you can be right about the psychological predictions that you're making.

If you can't think of any of your own theories to test, we've put together three that seem to be very popular and accurate among most people and the way that you can analyze those around you. These are important theories in making connections with other people, as well as persuading them should you have to in a certain scenario.

Priming

If you think of priming, you might commonly associate the term with painting. You pick out a primer to put on the walls before you decide to paint. This will ensure that the ugly mustard yellow the walls were painted before won't show through as you put a new coat of baby blue on. In psychological terms, priming is very similar to this idea.

This involves setting up conversations and actions for future preparation. This idea is most important in negotiations or moments of persuasion. Priming involves slipping words, images, and ideas into conversations before confronting the actual thing. Priming is used for people that don't like surprises, or those that aren't as willing to change.

Picture a husband and wife. Maybe the wife wants to have kids, but she isn't so sure her husband is ready. She knows that he reacts poorly to change and that when confronted, he tends to close himself off. It took her five years to get him to propose, so she needs to be careful about bringing up the baby conversation. She might start priming him by first putting on a movie about a baby. Maybe she'll make small comments here and there about wanting a baby or take detours through the baby sections at the local department stores. She'll want to prime him for the baby conversation, so he doesn't run and hide once she finally brings it up.

This type of behavior can be rather manipulative if not used for the right reasons. If the woman's husband had stated over and over again that he did not want children and never would change his mind, she shouldn't be priming him. However, there are some people that need a psychological push, and scaring the husband away wouldn't be the way to do so. The way that this behavior would be negatively manipulative is if someone is using it for personal gain only. If the change, or what is being primed, is going to benefit both parties, then it can be a useful tool in order to get what you want.

Amplification Hypothesis

The amplification hypothesis is one that involves heightening the excitement or negativity surrounding a certain subject. Many people probably use this sort of process without even realizing they are doing so. The process involves taking a subject, item, or other idea, and basically gassing it up, making it seem more exciting, and amplifying it to the next level. This involves either talking something down or building it up in order to alter perspectives.

Let's look at the husband and wife from the last section. She might decide to use this process by talking about how great babies are. Maybe she'll come home and discuss her friends' baby and how cute and perfect it was. She certainly won't mention that she still has puke on her shirt and instead only talk about the adorable noises and faces the baby made. Alternatively, the husband might amplify his hatred for children, if that's how he really feels. Maybe he'll point out a crying baby when they're in public, saying things like, "thank God we don't have kids."

The amplification hypothesis is usually true, but to use it isn't always the best option. Sometimes, it's better to just be honest about one's feelings and have a normal discussion without hidden meanings. This type of process can still be helpful for those that can't discuss things as openly as they'd like. When working on different projects in business or in your personal life, if you're working with others, there are going to be some group decisions that have to made. Sometimes, the amplification process can help you show your feelings without directly breaking down someone else's idea or saying anything that might hurt or offend another person.

The Scarcity Effect

The scarcity effect is the idea that when there is less of something, it can become more desirable. This is mostly thought of in sales. Think of the last store you went to. There were likely advertisements that said things like, "only two days left," "while supplies last," or "limited time only." Most of the time, this isn't true at all and are phrases only used to get people to buy quicker. This effect seriously works which is why so many businesses still use it. The same kind of effect can be made in different conversations and relationships. When trying to persuade someone, limiting the time or availability of an option can help sway them quicker.

Playing hard to get can help. While it's important to show vulnerability to others in order to make deeper connections, it's also important to maintain a certain distance. There's an idea that some people like "bad boys," and this is related to the scarcity effect. The idea that you can't have something makes people want it even more. The fear of regret that comes along with not getting something can be what drives a person to make a decision.

Think of a jar of cookies. If there are two jars, one completely filled and one with only three or four cookies left, most will go for the jar that's almost empty. They could be the same type of cookie, but most will assume that the jar that's almost empty has better tasting cookies. More people put their time and effort into eating the other cookies, so they probably have something better to offer.

Chapter 3 – Subliminal Persuasion

The idea of subliminal persuasion involves convincing someone to do something below their conscious level. You wouldn't blatantly persuade someone if you're being subliminal about it. Instead, you would try to convince them to do what you want without them even realizing what you're doing.

The idea of subliminal persuasion is mostly thought of in advertising. There are many companies that will do whatever they can to convince us to buy something, even if it means partially brainwashing us. The idea of subliminal persuasion doesn't have to be so insidious for those that wish to use these tactics to help persuade another person.

There are many important parts of subliminally persuading someone. You'll first want to make sure that you're doing it for the right reasons. You don't want to become someone that brainwashes others. It's not about getting into their head and tricking them into thinking something. Instead, you should be looking at what you know about them and using this in your plan for persuasion.

It's Not about Manipulation

You never want to make a person feel like they are crazy. You don't want to give sneaky hints that will make them question their own sanity. Subliminal persuasion should just be used as a nice way to tell someone how you really feel when you might be too scared to say the blatant truth.

Some people just have a harder time accepting truth,

persuasion, or reality than others. These types of people can't be blatantly told what someone else wants. Sometimes, people like to disagree with others just for the sake of being controversial. There are ways that you can take around obviously asking someone for something.

Subliminal persuasion should never be about manipulation. You shouldn't be "tricking" someone into something that will only benefit you. You should be using this method to try and better prevent against being subliminally persuaded yourself. It's also helpful for stubborn, intimidating, or other types of people that can't be so easily conversed with.

Confidence is Key

The trick to subliminally persuading someone is to exude as much confidence as possible. There are some people that will see overt confidence as delusional, so you don't want to take it too far. However, no one is going to be persuaded, no matter how subliminal you get, by someone that can't even stand up for their own thoughts and opinions.

Confidence is also important in order to distract the person from realizing that you might be trying to persuade them of something. Picture talking to your mom or dad, hoping to get to borrow the car again when you were a teenager. You would want to use some confidence, but not so much that you would want them to think you don't care about their permission. In order to subliminally persuade them, you might bring up the fact that there's no one else that can safely drive you to a party. Instead of blatantly asking and giving them the option to say no, instead, you're more able to sway them to your form of thinking. It can then become their own idea to let you borrow the car for the weekend.

Body Language Techniques

In the first chapter, many different body language theories were discussed, giving you insight into how or why someone uses their body in the way that they do. Using these same techniques is also important when it comes to subliminal persuasion. You'll want to show confidence, while also maintaining vulnerability, when trying to subliminally persuade someone.

Keep Speech Clear

An important part of subliminal persuasion is to actually speak clearly about what you want. Some people can be tricked if you speak quickly or use confusing words that they don't understand. This isn't fair and can be a form of negative manipulation.

Instead of trying to trick someone into giving you what you want, you can do it in a fair way that doesn't require confusing them. Plan out what you have to say if you must, but not too much. You don't want the conversation to feel like you're being too formal. Instead, pick out a few key points you feel are necessary, as well as some important words that you want to put emphasis on in your speech.

If someone can see that you're speaking with diction and confidence, they'll be more likely to agree to what you're asking than if you just trick them into saying yes by using confusing and jumbled language. That way, if something goes wrong later after the deal is made, you can remind them that you laid out the terms very clearly before they agreed.

Framing Conversations

Like we mentioned in the previous section, it can be incredibly helpful to lay out the framework for the conversations that you'll be having with others. You never want to write down exactly what you're going to say, as this will come off very static and obviously practiced. No one wants to respond well or say "yes" compassionately to a robot.

Framing is important because it helps build the foundation of your persuasion. You'll want to write down what your goals are, and how you're going to go about achieving those. It's also important to include the bumps and consequences you might face so you can properly prepare for those as well.

Choose Positivity

It can be hard to remain positive, especially when trying to persuade someone of something serious. Positivity almost always works better than using negativity, however. Frame your requests using positive words rather than negative ones. If you have to ask your parents to borrow $1,000, it can be nerve-wracking. Instead of using a negative explanation, such as, "I just lost my job and I'm behind on all my bills and don't know how I'm going to catch up," try being more positive, such as, "I only need $1000 because I'm in between jobs, but I applied to several new positions and know that the $1,000 is all I need to make sure I don't get behind!"

While both situations are tricky, your parents are going to see that they won't have as much risk with the second phrasing that they might face from the first scenario. It's the same situation. You're unemployed and you need money. However, you found the positivity in the second phrasing, showing your parents the hopefulness of the scenario as well. This is applicable in more ways than just asking someone for money.

Get people to start saying yes more. Instead of asking someone, "When are we going to set a date for the wedding?" try asking, "How does November first sound?" Instead of giving them the option to blow off the conversation, they have to confront the issue head-on. Don't give someone the option to avoid the conversation. Instead, think of a yes or no question that you can ask that can start leading the conversation.

Another example would be asking your roommate to have a party. You wouldn't want to say, "Can I have a party tomorrow?" This gives them the option to say no. Instead, try saying, "How about we have a party tomorrow night and then Sunday we can spend all day cleaning and relaxing." This puts the idea of the whole picture in their head so they're more likely to say yes, instead of making them confront an idea they might want to instantly say no to.

Plan Your Outcome

When writing a story, it's always best to think of the beginning, the middle, and the end, before you go on with writing the book. This way, you can include things in the beginning that might lead to hints as to what's going to happen in the end. How many times have you watched a movie, only to realize there were clues to who the murderer was all along!

This kind of planning is important to have in certain conversations as well. If you can plan what you want to gain from a specific interaction, you can include hints to that in the beginning of the conversation. This is an important way to prime as well as lay the framework for whatever your argument might be.

Physical Persuasion

How you physically look can be very persuasive for another person. Not everyone is physically large, so they might feel as though they can't stand up to others. It can be challenging to be a small person that has to stand up to those that are bigger!

At the same time, some people that are larger might feel like they have difficulty being vulnerable. They might feel as though all people see is their size, not giving them a chance thinking that they might be too tough or mean to approach.

There are ways around our own physical appearance that can help persuade other people. Even if someone is very large, they can still have meaningful connections not based around fear. Those that are smaller than most can still have a loud voice to help them stand up for themselves when they need to.

Choosing What to Wear

As much as most might not like to admit it, it can be important what we choose to wear, especially when making negotiations. The first step in choosing what is right to wear is to make sure that it's something you're comfortable in. This doesn't always mean sweatpants, but something that at least aligns with your personal style and clothing that you would actually be seen in. Others can tell when you might not be wearing something you would otherwise. A suit can look like a costume on someone that's normally in button-down shirts and slacks.

The next step is to make sure that it appropriately matches the occasion. Some people want to get as dressed up as possible, thinking their finest jewels and nicest threads will make them look better than most. You still want to make sure you're not overdoing it so that you can be approachable.

Color and patterns are important to consider as well. Warm colors can be inviting, but something that's too bold of a shade of red or yellow might also be a signal to be cautious for the other person. Blue and green can be welcoming colors as well, but you don't want to look like the ice king in too much baby blue. How someone responds to a color could be a direct indication of how they'll respond to your persuasion.

Scent is Important

Scent is much more persuasive than many people would think. There are some department stores that even release Christmas smelling scents around the holidays in order to elicit a happier mood that will cause people to spend more money!

When choosing a scent, it's important to wear something that matches your natural body scent. The samples you see for perfume at the store aren't just so you can smell the product.

It's also so you can try the scent out for a day and see how it mixes with the aromas you naturally give off. Perfume can be expensive but look at it as an investment towards persuasion and not just something that will make you smell nice.

NLP Tactics

NLP stands for neuro-linguistic programming. The idea is to look at the neurology, linguistics, and programming of a person to help determine what it is about them that makes them a unique individual.

Everyone has their own version of reality based around the way they were raised as well as the things they like. Once that reality is created, it can become a formula for how they handle different scenarios. NLP is discussed more in book one, so by this point, you should have a basic understanding of what it means.

Once you become aware of how someone else might be using NLP tactics on you, you can also use those tactics on other people as well.

Switching Up Physiology

Sometimes, switching up your physical space might be the exact thing that you need in order to use NLP to persuade or analyze another person. Maybe there's something blocking your way during the conversation. You might consider actually moving both you and the person you're talking to in order to create a more welcoming environment. If you feel like the conversation isn't going where you wanted, maybe take a bathroom break and give the person some time alone.

If you come back from the bathroom and things still are the same, suggest switching up the location. Maybe you could go for a walk or step out onto the patio. Sometimes, you don't always have to go this far. Perhaps just shifting your body movement or the way you're sitting is enough to re-engage the other person.

Visualization

Visualization is a great way for some people to achieve their goals. There are so many things that might seem out of reach, but you'd be surprised at how much you can accomplish if you just visualize what you want.

It can start by speaking something into existence. If you want to move to L.A. to become an actress, start talking about it. Don't tell people that you just want to do it at some point. Actually, say you're going to do it, and you'll be surprised at how much you can influence yourself towards these goals.

Write it down if you have to as well. This is more a method of self-persuasion than one that you can use on others, but it still certainly helps to speak and write about the goals and wishes you want to see fulfilled.

Taking Away the Ability to Say No

We briefly touched on this earlier but taking away the ability for another person to say no is an NLP tactic you can use for persuasion. Instead of saying, "Do you want to go out to dinner tonight?" ask someone, "Where are we going to dinner tonight?" You haven't given them the option to say no to your dinner date. They might say they can't anyway, but at least you tried to take away that option.

Instead of saying, "Can I have one?" say, "How many can I have?" Most people won't even realize that you've taken away their ability to turn you down.

Conclusion

This book should have provided you with a basic understanding of how to analyze and persuade those around you. While every individual is unique in their own way, there are certainly things that are similar between each and every person. Most of us have a desire to fulfill our own needs and wants, and when those ideas are realized, the person can be better analyzed. How a person was raised and the environment that they grew up in is very important in determining what it is that makes a person unique.

When analyzing another person, it starts with looking at their body language. Do they hold themselves high or do they hide behind their own body? How a person uses their eyes, face, and arms, are the most important parts of determining what they might really be like. You can realize that someone who seems confident might actually be debilitated by their anxiety if you start to notice the way they hold themselves. You could also discover that someone you thought you could trust is actually deceiving you.

It can be hard to pinpoint what it is about a person that separates them from others, and why they might act the way they do. You'll never have a complete understanding of another person, but you will at least be able to start to realize why they might act the way they do.

Once you've been able to analyze someone, you can then start to persuade them. This is important in some cases to get what you want, or at the very least, get what you deserve. Just as we discussed in book one, you can read this over and over again, but unless you take action, nothing is going to change. It can be hard to start to become aware of yourself, but it's a key step in becoming aware of those around you.

Once you have the ability to analyze yourself and others, you'll be able to better persuade and convince them as well. When you can do this, you'll realize all the power you have over your own life.

James W. Williams

Persuasion

Dark Psychology

How People are Influencing You to do What They Want Using Manipulation, NLP, and Subliminal Persuasion

Introduction

It's never easy to feel like you might be getting taken advantage of. Whether it's a spouse, a friend, a relative, a child, a sibling, or even just the person that makes your coffee in the morning, anyone is capable of taking advantage of other people.

In the same way, anyone is at risk for being the person that is getting manipulated. Even the most powerful people might be under the influence of someone else's manipulation. Having control over another person is a very powerful feeling, and some people use this as their life source. Other people have been so controlled by others throughout their lives that they don't have an identity other than the one of their abuser.

This book aims to break apart three main ways that someone might be getting taken advantage of. There will be examples of how to identify this type of manipulation, and what can be done to stop and prevent further toxic behavior.

The first step in the recovery process is understanding manipulative behavior at its core. It's important to figure out what a manipulator looks like, and how they might specifically take advantage of other people. By understanding this you're better equipped to identify and defend against the manipulation.

This book isn't going to be about how to use these techniques on others to manipulate them. Manipulation is dangerous and it's crucial to understand the damage that this tool can do. Many people live unhappy lives because they have been so manipulated by others. It's time for that deception to end, and instead, you should be putting focus on improving relationships and overall self-esteem.

This book will also focus more on 1 on 1 persuasion, but it's still important to understand that there are certain medias that are taking advantage of you as well. Manipulation surrounds us, and it seems inescapable. While the manipulation won't ever fully stop, there are ways of preventing it from happening, and methods of attacking just how much it affects a person's life.

Just because someone is a victim of manipulation doesn't mean they might not also be a manipulator themselves. Often, the two go hand in hand. It's tricky behavior, but if more is known about it, there will be a better understanding of how to stop this toxic pattern.

Chapter 1 – Manipulation

Manipulation involves the emotional exploitation and distortion of one's mental processes in order to receive something that the manipulator wants. In certain abusive situations, it can sometimes be obvious that there is some form of harm being done. Manipulation is much trickier to identify, and many people will go a long time without realizing that they are being manipulated.

Everyone has likely manipulated someone else in their life. It's just a part of our average conversations and interactions. Sometimes, you might persuade someone to do something because you have an ulterior motive. Maybe you hear that your friend's going to be out of town for your birthday party, so you tell them how much fun it's going to be, hoping that they'll skip their trip. Though this isn't that harmful, it can be considered manipulation.

Manipulation starts in childhood. That can be how many of us learn how to get what we want. Children are master manipulators, attempting to alter the truth, their feelings, and the emotions of their parents in order to get what they want. It's part of our childhood development. At some point, kids realize that they can't hurt people to get what they want, and as empathy develops, it's much easier to become less manipulative.

Manipulation can turn into a form of abuse when it is not properly monitored. There are people that grow well into adulthood, still manipulating the people around them. Some manipulators don't realize what they're doing while others might rely on this tactic to get what they want. Manipulation is very complex, and this chapter will unpack the basic understanding of manipulation.

Where Manipulation is Found

Manipulation occurs mostly within the closest relationships of another person. Spouses, parents and children, siblings, and relationships amongst best friends can become very manipulative. The people that surround us are the ones we look to when in need. We see our family and friends as those that provide us with something, at least to a certain extent. When some feel as though they might be in need of something that they can't easily get, they begin to manipulate a situation.

It can also be seen in the workplace often. Bosses might manipulate their employees in order to get what they need to reach a certain goal. Coworkers might manipulate one another in order to get ahead, often competing for positions that might change the overall fate of their lives.

Manipulation is also in the society around us. The way advertisers use our fears to make us buy certain things. The way political campaigners try to gain voters. These processes can become incredibly manipulative. The majority of this book will discuss one on one interactions, but it's important to be aware of how manipulative commercials, billboards, radio ads, and print media can be. There are many tactics that big companies use to get consumers to buy into certain ideas. This manipulation can be powerful, but when one becomes aware of the manipulation around them in their personal lives, they have an easier time of recognizing it in social settings as well.

Profile of a Manipulator

There are certain qualities that all manipulators have. Each and every person that has manipulated in their lives is different, however, the characteristics that make us manipulate are usually similar. There are certain reasons a person might become a manipulator. It might have been in their household, and the way that they were raised. Often, children of drug addicts end up becoming manipulators later in life, learning how to lie and deceive at an alarmingly early age.

A manipulator might have formed their habits later in life, covering up their own addiction or fear of failing. Manipulators might have learned that they can get what they want if they influence people in a certain way. Some individuals seem to have a certain charm to them while others couldn't lie to save their life. Manipulation is insidious, and the pattern of behavior can be incredibly hard to break.

This next section will go over what a manipulator looks like. Sometimes, you might have to do some looking inward. Not everyone wants to admit it, but there's a good chance that they might partake in some manipulation themselves. Even victims of abuse might manipulate, perhaps lying to friends and family about the level of violence they endure. Not all manipulators are bad, but the behavior itself is something that should be avoided.

Whoever a manipulator might be, they usually have a reason

why they wish to take advantage of others. Those that manipulate aren't always aware, but they will have a certain goal that they are working towards.

Manipulation Motives

The biggest reason someone might be a manipulator is because they want to have a sense of control. They might have come from an unstable childhood, never finding a sense of self. They then struggle to identify themselves, feeling as though they don't have control over their lives. Some people will internalize this pain, becoming codependent on other people acting passively. Other people will be more active with their codependency, gaining a false sense that they can have control over their own lives if they can control others. They'll then manipulate a situation, attempting to have power over ones around them.

A manipulator will do whatever it takes to make someone else have a certain perception of them. As humans develop, they start to make certain perceptions of what is good or bad, desirable and avoidable. People start to develop standards for certain aspects of life, and if they feel as though they're lacking in any way, they might choose to manipulate their reality. Manipulators usually have low self-esteem. They'll lie about how late they slept in to try to make others think they're more of a hard worker.

Criminal advantages could be why someone is manipulative as well. Drug addicts might manipulate their family into thinking they need money for rent or other bills, when really they need it for drugs. They might tell a family member that they're sick and the drugs are the only thing that makes them better. A thief will lie to their friends and family about where they're getting their money. They'll manipulate the truth to others around them, sometimes involving them in the crime, just to have control over the situation.

Everyone has their own reasons why they might be manipulating others, but being the victim is never easy. Manipulators will stop at nothing to get what they want, whether it's money, fame, drugs, or power. Sometimes, those closest to us end up being our master manipulators. The entire situation is difficult, especially when there is an imbalance of how much is being taken versus how much is received.

What Happens to the Victim

A victim of a manipulator will often feel codependent on the person that has been influencing them. Those that manipulate often might be abusive towards someone close to them. The victim of a manipulator will have a false sense of power. They see the manipulator as the one in charge, the one who knows best. They've been made to feel like they have no power, so they end up looking to the manipulator for help, validation, and purpose.

They will start to doubt their own thoughts and feelings. The manipulator has repeatedly made them feel as though they don't have any value. They will convince the victim that they have no worth in order to invalidate their thoughts and feelings. They don't want the victim to have any power because they need to feel like they are in control. The victim sees themselves as worthless, the other person holding all the value. They will start to wonder why their opinions matter at all. They will identify their own thoughts and emotions with that of the manipulator.

Manipulators often have trouble admitting they are in their current situation. If a victim does recognize what's going on, they usually have to be incredibly careful with how they approach the manipulator. They might use scare tactics in order to keep their victims submissive. Manipulators will not be the first ones to come forward about the abuse of power, as that would be admitting their vulnerability. Once it is identified, it can feel helpless to break free.

It's important for those that feel as though they might be manipulated to gain their voice back. It can be scary, but it can certainly be done. The first step is knowing what makes a manipulator and identifying with how they handle their own thoughts and emotions. Not everyone will be able to confront their manipulation, but many friends, relatives, and partners can overcome their imbalance of power.

Profile of a Gas Lighter

A gas lighter is a type of manipulator that makes the victim question their form of reality. They will say things like "you're remembering it wrong," "you're always so hung up on this," or, "you're acting crazy!" Gas lighters will be the first ones to tell someone that they're overreacting. When confronted with the idea that they might be gaslighting, they will usually become angry and defensive, unwilling to at least confront the thought that they might be exhibiting less than perfect behavior.

The term started popping up around 1944 after a movie about

a man that tries to convince his wife she's insane became popular. The movie, *Gaslight*, was about a woman, Paula, that married a man, Gregory, and moved to the secluded home of her aunt after her murder. Paula starts to worry when things go missing and strange things start happening in her home, her husband Gregory telling her that she's going insane and imagining it all. One thing included her noticing the gaslight go on at night, her husband claiming she was just imagining it. All along, Gregory had been deceiving her, and was the actual murderer of Paula's aunt. The term caught on and began referring to any situation in which one person makes another feel as though they are insane.

Gas lighters continue this unhealthy behavior in order to gain something from the victim. They might be covering up a lie. A man that's cheating on his girlfriend will tell her she's acting crazy if she questions where he has been. A teenage girl might tell her mother that she's crazy for wondering where she was, even though that girl was at a party she wasn't supposed to be at. A friend might tell the other they're being dramatic if that friend brings up something that emotionally hurt them.

Gas lighters will not admit that they are wrong, and when they are confronted with an opposing view, they'll redirect that suspicions onto the other person. Instead of admitting their own flaws, they'll do their best to turn the attention to their opponent's shortcomings. Gas lighters are dangerous manipulators that should be treated with caution.

Subtle Manipulation

Manipulation isn't always so blatantly obvious. While some

victims don't even realize they're being manipulated, there are many manipulators that don't realize what they're doing either. There are some obvious forms of manipulation, but there are also many more subtle versions that not everyone will always notice. This kind can be tricky, and often so insidious that it can be hard to recover.

If the manipulator is in a bad mood, then they might make everyone around them miserable as well. Manipulators might sit in the corner, purposely acting sad in order to gain the attention of others. Someone more active might even go as far as to bring the other people around them down in order to make everyone as miserable as them. They'll take whatever kind of attention they can get, even if that means it's negative.

Manipulators might also exaggerate their illness or injury in order to gain more attention. They might use their illness as an excuse for certain parts of their behavior. While there are plenty of ill people that do have legitimate reasons, when they do certain things, it all depends on if someone else is negatively affected. A manipulator that's ill might act rudely to someone, using their illness as an excuse for their hurtful behavior.

Sometimes, it can be hard to determine if someone's being manipulative or not. It's not as if a person is going to admit right away that they're being manipulative. Once it is recognized, it can be even harder to figure out how to come up with a solution to get over the problem. There are certain tactics that most manipulators use in order for them to get what they want.

Manipulation Tactics

This section will take you through common manipulation tactics, starting with less serious and moving on towards more harmful forms. Everyone has experienced manipulation differently, but there are certain things that are true in most cases. What makes a manipulator choose to influence people is always going to be different, but how they do it is similar in different cases.

Some manipulators have exhibited behavior like this all their lives. Their parents might have been the first ones to introduce them to the tactics it takes to manipulate other people. It can be rather devastating to have to revisit childhood, but many people will find that their manipulation behaviors stem from the things they learned as kids. Manipulation might have been a survival tool for some, the only way they knew how to satisfy any of their needs. For others, manipulation might have come from a sibling that felt inferior. Maybe they now look to manipulation as a way to get people to like them, or at least alter their perception.

Other manipulators might only have a few of the common traits found in those that take advantage of others. Even someone that seems like a genuine, caring, and loving person might still be a manipulator to someone in their life. They might even overcompensate for their behavior with others because they're aware of their poor treatment on a certain person in their life.

Manipulation can be tricky to spot, but it's crucial to do so in order to stop the cycle. What is blatant manipulation to one person might be a way of life for the other. We all have different experiences that account for various aspects of our life, but it's important to always be aware of the way we interact with ourselves and others in order to continually improve our quality of life.

Humor Aimed at Your Weaknesses

Some manipulators will use humor in order to mask their deception. They'll make little jokes here and there that seem harmless but have deep-rooted intentions of manipulation. They'll joke about things they might know that you're sensitive about, or perhaps things to make you feel like less of a person. The manipulator is attempting to make you feel less than them. They're belittling you to make you feel small and to attempt to build themselves up.

These might include subtle jokes like, "It's nice to see that you actually got out of bed today." They are attempting to make a person feel as though they sleep too late on a regular basis. Or a deeper jab like, "Your hair looks nice for once." You'll be blindsided by the compliment, only to then realize that they managed to insult you every other day that they'd seen you. Manipulators will often make these jokes in front of a group of people as well to really diminish your credibility with your friends and family.

They'll then usually make you feel as though it's not fair to get upset over their humor. They'll say things like, "Learn to take a joke," or, "Just laugh at yourself." Manipulators will want to make it feel as though you're in the wrong for being sensitive over the joke. They'll want you to believe that you are the one with the problem and they did nothing wrong.

Manipulators will make other people the butt of the joke in an attempt to approve their self-esteem. They'll attempt to point out someone else's flaw just so they don't have to look at their own. Someone that has insecurities about their weight might make jokes about someone else's, hoping that those around them forget about the state of the manipulator.

There is a grasp at power here. The person being manipulated will feel as though they no longer have any value. They'll be made to see themselves as a joke. Any feelings or sensitivities they have over these jokes will become meaningless to the victim. They'll feel like their own thoughts don't matter, believing everything that the manipulator said about their insecurity.

Surprise and Little Time

A manipulator might use the pressure of time in order to influence other people. They'll make them feel as though they have to rush to have a final decision in a situation that would normally require more time.

Giving a person little time to make a decision puts a lot of pressure on them. They feel stressed and nervous, depending on the aggressor in order to feel a sense of relief. The manipulator then gets what they wanted all along.

Surprise is another manipulation tactic that is often used. A manipulator will attempt to overload their victim with something that's hard to process. They then won't have time for the proper response, so the manipulator wins.

Imagine two people in a relationship, one wanting to buy a new car and the other consistently denying that request. The manipulator might show up with a new car, not giving the other person any time to have a proper reaction. It was such a big purchase that the one who didn't want the car feels as though they now have to give in. What other choice do they have?

By not allowing enough time for a proper reaction, a manipulator is deciding how their victim is going to feel for them. They give them no other choice but to submit to the manipulator.

Lying About and Exaggerating Facts

A manipulator will often exaggerate the truth in order to convince the other person of what might benefit the aggressor. They might say something like, "I could go to the store, but traffic was really bad earlier, so it might be a while," even though they know traffic was at a normal level. They'll take the truth and stretch it as far as they have to in order to convince those around them of the lie, they need to cover themselves. They will say what they have to in order to get the other person off their back.

A manipulator will take any small piece of information and exploit it to the maximum. If their leg hurts after helping a friend move, they'll make sure to bring that pain up as much as possible in order to make their help look like more than it was. They might also say something at one point, completely lying and saying the opposite later. They'll be so detached from reality that they won't be afraid to blatantly lie about the things they may or may not have said.

Manipulators will also straight up lie about the truth. They might say that they were studying all night, when really they were cheating on their girlfriend. They might say that they hadn't done drugs in a month while high. Manipulators will stop at nothing to make someone else believe whatever they have to in order to reach their goals. They aren't afraid of being caught in a lie either, because they'll just lie their way out of that. Some manipulators are so bad that they'll use every tool at their disposal just to cover up one little lie.

Some manipulators are so far into their delusions that they'll end up believing the lie. They won't even react normally when confronted because they'll legitimately believe they did or didn't do what they're being accused of. They are shameless in their lying because they actually end up believing their delusions.

Giving You the Upper Hand

A manipulator will make you feel as though you're in charge. They'll give the illusion that you have the power in the situation. They'll try to tell you what to do but then say things like, "but you're in charge," so that if something does go wrong, the manipulator won't be blamed.

A manipulator might let you speak first, making you believe that you're in control of the situation. You might end up realizing that they only did this in order to hear your weaknesses first and build their argument. They'll give you the chance to state your argument first, but instead of actually listening to your thoughts and feelings, they'll just be meticulously planning their next manipulation.

Manipulators will ask you questions with the impression that they're compassionate. Instead of listening to your answers, they're actually forming their own responses to use against you. They'll trick you into thinking they're listening, but they're actually just breaking apart what you're saying in order to use it against you. They'll listen closely and even take exact phrases of what you said, twisting them and using them against you later.

A manipulator might invite you to their home when discussing something, using this power balance to their advantage. They'll make you believe they're being hospitable even though they are trying to gain the upper hand themselves.

Manipulation as a Positive

Not all manipulation has to be bad. There is certainly a negative connotation surrounding the word manipulation. It is often associated with abusive people that only take advantage of others. That is certainly true in a way, as most abusers use manipulation tactics to get what they want. More often than not, in fact, examples of manipulation turn out to be negative. Not every instance of manipulation has to be negative, however. There are certain ways that manipulation can be used positively.

Think of it like a tool. Manipulation is similar to a hammer. You can either use it to destroy something or create something new. The act of having control is a very powerful position. That power can either be used for good, or it can be used for bad. If you know the password to someone's computer, you can use that to login and look at their information, or you can simply ignore it. If you find a wallet in a bathroom, you can take the cash and toss the wallet, or you can turn it into the front desk. If you know someone's weaknesses, you can use that to exploit them, or you can help improve their life, encouraging them when they feel weak.

Most will use manipulation to their advantage, and this is dangerous behavior. It's important to recognize that not everyone who exhibits manipulative behavior is using it negatively. Some people see manipulation as a survival tactic. They might manipulate others because they legitimately think they know what's best. Many children are manipulative, but not because they're evil. Children are just figuring out how to interact with other people, and the way our actions have power over others is important to discover and dissect.

Positive Social Influence

Social influence is the way in which our society, and the people around us, has developed ideals to influence the individuals in those institutions. Social norms, religion, morality, and ethics all influence how we interact and shape our own personal views. Social influence is derivative from three varieties. The first is compliance, which involves keeping your opinions to yourself, even if they're different from others. The second is identification, which is the influence from someone that is respected and admired. The third is internalization, which is when an idea, behavior, or belief is accepted, and everyone agrees privately as well as publicly.

Social influence can be harmful, but there are also instances in which it can be positive. An example might be a doctor using their persuasion to make their clients believe a certain thing. They'll believe a disease is best treated with a certain medication, so they'll manipulate their patient to take that, with no ulterior motives or attempt at personal gain.

There might also be campaigns directed towards educating users on certain things that need to be changed in society. For example, think of the commercials that are aimed towards getting people to quit smoking. They can be very manipulative in behavior, sometimes exaggerating certain truths and using fear tactics. This manipulation isn't aimed at anything other than trying to benefit both parties.

Not All Manipulators are Evil

If someone is identified as being a manipulator, that doesn't mean that they're automatically evil. Everyone has different reasons why they might be attempting to manipulate those around them. There are always better ways to confront issues than to use manipulation tactics, but sometimes, this is all someone knows. They might not be aware of how to properly express their emotions, so instead they'll use manipulation tactics to try and get what they want.

Think of it like a girl that sees her sister struggling in every aspect of her life. Maybe the sister is failing her classes, addicted to alcohol, and avoiding paying her bills. The girl might use manipulation tactics to try to get her sister to improve her behavior. She's not necessarily evil, she just wants what's best for her sister, and maybe believes tricking her into doing something is going to provide a better result for both of them.

Manipulation is usually a form of avoiding a bigger truth. Maybe humor is used by a wife to joke about her husband's hair, when really, she should just be honest and say that he needs a haircut. The husband might not agree, but at least he won't be made to feel like less than himself by his wife's cruel humor. While not everyone that uses manipulation is necessarily bad, they should still try to confront the bigger issue at hand before using deceptive tactics on their loved ones.

Overcome Manipulation

Once manipulation is identified, the next step is to get through it. Overcoming manipulation can be very challenging. In some cases, a 60 year-old-man might realize just now that his 85 year-old-mother is manipulative. They might never get through their issues, but they should still be confronted. Manipulation takes a part of both the abuser and the victim. It can ruin people's lives, altering the direction they take and affecting the rest of their years. Manipulation can be hard to identify and even harder to overcome.

It can be done, and it should be attempted to get through. In a relationship based around manipulation, there might not be any coming back. Sometimes, people might just have to break up. You might have to get a divorce or stop calling your mom. It takes two people to partake in a manipulative scenario. Not both people will end up identifying it as a manipulative situation, however. In that case, the person that realizes what's actually going on might just have to move on, the manipulator never realizing the damage they caused.

This can be a challenging part of overcoming manipulation. Usually, some instance of codependency formed, making it even harder to break away. There are ways to overcome this, and we will cover that in the next few sections.

Know Your Worth

The first step in overcoming manipulation is for the victim to identify that they still have value. A manipulator likely took everything from their victim. They belittled them, ridiculed them, and made them feel as though what they thought didn't matter. In some situations, they might have even used gaslighting tactics to make their victims feel as though they're insane. It can be hard for a victim to then recognize just how much value they still have once they become aware of the manipulation.

It's important for everyone to know, no matter who is reading this, that you have worth. Everyone has value. No one deserves to be manipulated. No one deserves to feel as though they don't have any purpose, reason, or value. You have the right to be treated justly, and with respect from other people. You are allowed to express your emotions, feelings, wants, and opinions. No one else has the right to tell you how to feel. You set your own boundaries, and no one else gets to decide for you.

If you feel sad about something, that is completely valid. No one gets to decide if what they say hurts you or not. Not everyone might intentionally mean to hurt you, but that doesn't mean you're not allowed to still feel bad. You have the right to feel the way you do, and you have the same right to express those beliefs.

If you feel like you need to protect yourself, you are just in doing so. If you feel like your safety is being threatened, or someone is taking advantage of you, you have the right to remove yourself from that situation without guilt. No one gets to treat you badly, and though that can be hard for many of us to hear, it's the truth.

Manipulators aim to take these thoughts away. They want to deprive their victims of their rights in order to work towards getting what they want. This can't happen anymore. It's up to the manipulator's victims to now recognize their worth and stop the cycle of manipulation.

Don't Be Afraid to Keep Your Distance

Many people that feel as though they're being manipulated end up being too afraid to do anything about it. They have been stripped of their own thoughts and opinions, their own feelings invalidated and instead focus on how other people feel. Those that have been continually manipulated might be afraid to leave those that have hurt them. They've depended on those that abused them for so long they don't know where else to go.

You're allowed to keep your distance. You don't have to feel guilty about protecting yourself. It can be hard to separate yourself from a manipulator, especially in a romantic relationship. You might see the very weaknesses that cause their manipulative behavior. Maybe in a relationship, a boyfriend's dad was an abusive alcoholic, and it greatly hurt him. It also caused his violent manipulative behavior that led him to hitting his girlfriend on a few occasions. It's true that he has his own pain, but that doesn't mean he's allowed to inflict it on others. The girlfriend has every right to leave her boyfriend and find her own peace and protection.

Ask what is really lost by leaving the person that's manipulating you. More often than not, value in a relationship is placed on codependent tendencies. A person is afraid to leave not because they love their manipulator, but because they are afraid to be alone. It can be scary to be on your own, but mostly because manipulators put that idea in their victims in the first place. Manipulators will trick their victims into staying with them because deep down, they know that the victim will be just fine without them.

It's Not Your Job to Change Them

Once manipulation is recognized, the next step is to try to talk to the person about the manipulation. It's time to get down to the root issues of the relationship and figure out what can be done to help both partners get what they need, instead of just the manipulator. There has been an imbalance of power for far too long, and it's time to rebalance.

Unfortunately, not many manipulators are willing to admit their faults and later change their behavior. Instead, they'll do whatever they can to distract others from their faults, placing the blame on their victims instead. When this happens, the victim has to accept that their manipulator isn't going to change, and they must find the strength to leave.

There will likely be a desire to change the other person and help them improve their life as well. Not everyone will always be on the same page of their journey towards self-discovery. It can be hard to accept for some victims, but they have to realize that it's not their job to change their manipulator.

You can only help a person so much, and if they're not willing to change or improve themselves, it's not going to happen. Many people wait around for the other to change in their relationship, hoping their manipulation will get better. If a person isn't aware of their behavior and aren't actively trying to change it, nothing is going to happen in the end.

Confronting the Manipulator

By this point, there should be a comprehensive understanding of what a manipulator is, why they might be manipulative, and what the common tactics of manipulation are. Once this identification has been made, the next step is to move on from the unhealthy cycle that has manifested.

This will usually involve confronting the manipulator. Often, the manipulator might not be aware of what they're doing. There's a good chance that if a conversation is attempted and an actual discussion starts, a person will realize what they have done and might actually try to improve on their manipulative behavior.

Other times, a person might become very defensive, not wanting to admit it to the people that they have hurt. Some people won't be strong enough to recover because they don't want to have to look into themselves and admit their flaws. They've spent so much time internalizing their own self-hate that they aren't capable of confronting the truth. Part of overcoming manipulation is accepting that it's okay to be flawed. Many people have done things that have hurt others, but that doesn't mean all hope is lost.

Sometimes, manipulators are so abusive that they won't be able to come down from their power trip at all. These people should be handled with caution. If a confrontation might lead to physical abuse, it should be avoided, or only done in the presence of others so as to avoid violence. Every manipulator is different, but there are some tactics that can be used to help stop the manipulation in its tracks.

Ask Questions

When manipulation is detected, it's important to start asking questions. Those start with the victim asking themselves questions first. Question whether or not you're being treated with respect. Is what this person asking of you fair? Are they putting you in a position that they know makes you uncomfortable? Is there a big imbalance of power in the relationship?

Once this is done, the victim of the manipulation will be able to easily identify if they are being taken advantage of. They can then form the basis for their confrontation in order to have a healthy and productive conversation with the person that was being manipulative in the first place.

It is also helpful to ask the manipulator questions when they might be trying to influence others. A victim of manipulation might ask their abuser if their request seems reasonable. Would they ask the same thing of another person? Would they do the same work themselves? Is the person being asked, or are they being demanded? Do they actually have a choice in the matter?

By asking these important questions, a mirror is created, and the manipulator is forced to look at themselves. They have to see what they're doing to their victim, and in a way, they are being confronted with the truth. They might not have even asked these things of themselves, so it might not be until now that they realize how much damage they have been doing.

Take Your Time

The manipulator might use tactics of speed or time pressure to get what they want. This is done in order to distract their victims and not give them a chance to really think everything over.

By taking your time, you allow an opportunity to really make the right decision. You make the manipulator know that you aren't going to be scared into saying yes or no. If you're not sure what to say, always just tell the manipulator that, "you'll think about it." This is not giving them a definitive yes or no. It's letting them know that you're actually going to put time into analyzing the request, deciding if it's something that's actually going to be good for you or not. Many people will be afraid to say this, as they don't want to upset anyone else. You have to know that your feelings take priority, and anyone that is really rushing you for an answer might have manipulation motives.

Many jobs and bosses will use speed tactics to get what they want. They'll offer you a position with a certain salary but tell you that you need to decide quick, so they can let someone else know if they got the job. Anyone that tries to sell something will use time pressure, making the person questioning their purchase know that others might buy it up first. This kind of manipulative tactic works well, but if it's there, it's usually best to just take your time in making a decision.

Practice Saying No

Something that can be incredibly challenging for victims of manipulation is the ability to say no. Manipulators usually make those around them feel as if saying no isn't even an option. They'll make them believe that if they say no, they'll lose something. Manipulators are all about taking from others, so of course, they're skilled at forcing people to say yes as often as possible. They'll use guilt, shame, and embarrassment to force someone to give in. When it comes to overcoming manipulative scenarios, it's crucial to say no when needed.

Saying no can be very powerful. Telling someone that you're not available, what they're asking makes you uncomfortable, or that you just have to say no isn't easy, but it's crucial in overcoming manipulative scenarios. Saying no sets boundaries. It lets others know what you're comfortable with and what you're not. Saying no is sometimes about trusting your gut. Those that have been manipulated for long periods of time no longer trust their gut. They've been made to feel as though what they think and feel is invalid. It's important for them to get back to a place that they can rely on the feelings in their stomach. No one should be put through an uncomfortable scenario because they're too afraid to say no.

If someone is mad that you said no, they probably weren't good for you in the first place. Some people will find that if they start saying no more often, they'll lose a friend, or a certain person will stop talking to them. While it can be scary to be alone, this is actually a good thing. It helps a person realize who is a real friend and who was just there because they knew they could get them to say yes.

Chapter 2 – NLP

Richard Bandler John Grinder developed the idea of NLP in Santa Cruz in 1976. NLP stands for neurolinguistic programming; neuro focusing on neurology, linguistics referencing language, and programming referring to the function of that neural language. These men studied three individual's abilities to change their thoughts and feelings. Many people have adopted their ideas, though criticism still remains around the legitimacy of their study results.

NLP should be thought of not as a process to use on other people, but on yourself. The basic idea of NLP is to change the thoughts and feelings of oneself. Doing this can relieve anxiety, depression, and other mental illnesses. They might feel as though a certain thought or belief holds them back, and by changing one's feelings on this, they can change their life. An example would be a person that decides to make themselves believe they like exercising. Some people have found success in using NLP tactics, though many people have criticized the capabilities of the process as well.

There are certainly some benefits to neurolinguistic programming, but many people use this as a manipulation tactic. The intention of NLP tactics is to be able to look into oneself to figure out what makes them an individual. What forms a person's beliefs can also indicate their quality of life. By changing these beliefs, they can improve a certain aspect of their life. Some manipulators use NLP tactics to convince others to do things that will benefit the manipulator.

In order to understand how someone might be using NLP to manipulate you, it's important to first understand what exactly NLP tactics are. There is some positivity in this way of thinking, so even those that don't find this in their lifestyle in the form of manipulation might still benefit by following this thought process.

How We Receive Information

Our worlds are created based around what we put focus on. What we put our energy into will build the foundations for which we think, feel, express, love, work, and do everything else in our lives that makes us an individual. A person that lives in Beverly Hills has a much different world than someone from the middle of nowhere in Texas. While both are humans born in the United States, they live much different lives, with varying perspectives, beliefs, and morals. You only notice what you tune in on.

Your own world is different than the one around you. For example, someone could go their entire lives not realizing how many car dealerships are on their normal route to work. They might take the same streets to the same place, day after day, week after week, year after year, never realizing they pass three car dealerships. Then the time comes when their car breaks down, and they have to buy a car. Once buying a car becomes that person's goal, they suddenly realize its relevance in the world.

This is often why people will see "signs." Signs are usually our minds just looking for outside validation for something that we want. Perhaps someone is considering whether or not they should have a child. Maybe they see a woman holding a baby on the bus, and then another time they notice a baby commercial. This person considering whether or not to have children might take these as "signs," when really, they signaled their brain once the dilemma started. Their subconscious became alert of all things baby, trying to pick up on signs all around them to help answer whether or not they should have a child.

Some people could go their entire lives without realizing there's something right in front of their face, and then one day, there's a trigger that awakens their newfound alertness.

Your Personality Profile

This is what helps us determine what information we're going to store. What are your interests, what are your hobbies? What are your pet peeves? What makes your skin crawl? What keeps you up at night? What do you hope for the future? These important questions, the ones that make us unique individuals, are what make up our personality profiles.

We all have our own agenda. Whether you're aware or not, you have a reason that you do what you do. If you want to be wealthy, you look for ways that you can make and save money. If you don't want to work but want money, you might find ways to take advantage of other people to get what you want. Everyone has a different motive, agenda, reason.

Goals can be as general as wanting to be rich, or as specific as wanting to be the ultimate pizza eating champion of a small town in Missouri. Some people are very aware of their goals and actively try to contribute to their goal progression on a daily basis. Others aren't quite sure of their motives and continue to go through life based on basic survival tactics.

Your personality profile determines how you take in information and what you end up doing with that. The main forms of consumption, such as social media, television, and other dark corners of the internet, play into our personality profiles. The thoughts and beliefs our friends and family share with us contribute to our personality profile. Even our physical descriptions, whether we're fit or fat, masculine or feminine, old or young, all contribute to our personality profile as well.

The Animalistic Nature of Our Brain

When deciding to take in the things around us, there are certain questions we start to ask. Is this safe or not? That can be the first instinct for many people, even those that aren't as aware. They might sense danger, whether it's from a shady person or not wanting to live in a specific area of a neighborhood.

Does this have value? This is another question we consider when making decisions. Putting value on certain things differs from person to person, but there is some level of questioning something's worth when presented with making a decision.

Does this help me accomplish something? Is this job, relationship, tool, or other idea meeting some of our needs?

These needs and wants are derivative of our biology. We want money because we want to buy food because if we don't eat, we'll die. This is an obvious one. A subtler natural reaction of our brain is our desire to fit in. When we lived in a world where forming groups was necessary for survival, we developed an urge to prove our worth. A normal "tribe" would have hunters, gatherers, security, and other roles necessary for the survival of everyone. Not everyone was a hunter or a gatherer, but everyone had their worth and they would do what they had to in order to prove their value.

We still have this desire, but it reflects in different ways. We want to prove we have value, so people keep us around, but some people end up mistaking that. A woman might get breast implants to prove that she's beautiful, and she puts value on her beauty. A man might sleep with hundreds of women in order to prove his masculinity.

When we understand our natural biology, that urge that exists in everyone to prove their worth, it can be easier to start to redirect our thoughts.

Our Map of Reality

What everyone around them perceives is completely different. Even a set of twins could have an opposite outlook on life. It's more likely that two people from different geographical or religious backgrounds would have different viewpoints. Still, those that are from seemingly similar places might have completely different perspectives on what reality might look like.

Social influences play a huge part in how a person acts and develops. The background of the people in a community can affect everyone. If most people come from affluent backgrounds, they will all have similar perspectives, forming the viewpoints of those that grow and function in that specific area. If more people are involved in crime in a certain area, it's likely that lifestyle will affect others around. It isn't true for everyone, but location can play a huge role in how a person thinks.

The biological makeup of a person is very important as well. Someone with a family history of anxiety and depression will directly affect their personality and the way they interact with other people. Biological influences beyond just the wiring of our brain play an important part in the mapping of our reality as well. Beyond just mental genetics, hair, skin, and eye color can play into a person's personality, thought processes, and beliefs as well.

Whether nature or nurture plays a more important role is a highly debated topic. It's likely that there is a blend of both that vary from person to person that affect how someone thinks. The family a person was born into, and how they were raised after birth, both greatly affect how a person will act and think throughout their entire lives.

Meaning is Subjective

Since our realities are so different, meaning will become varied as well. Some think the meaning of life is to serve a higher power, such as a god or set of gods. Others think the meaning is to find happiness, while some don't think there's any meaning at all. Our personality profiles, animalistic behaviors, genetic biology, and social upbringing will end up defining our own individual meaning.

Meaning is also subjective because it can be altered at any one time. Someone could go their entire lives believing in God, eventually deciding they're atheist. The opposite could happen too. Some people think they'll never lose their faith, or gain faith, but end up surprised at how quickly they can change their thoughts.

Religion is so tricky because no one was born believing one thing. They might have always felt a certain spirituality deep down, but the major parts of Buddhism, Muslimism, and Christianity were all things that were taught. Meaning is taught to us in a certain aspect, but we also create our own definitions and meanings as well.

The meaning of life might never be clearly defined for every individual, but everyone has their own ideas on what's most important in their life. If they don't, that ends up affecting how they think and act as well. There's power in knowing that you can change your mind at any time, but unfortunately, not everyone will realize this freedom in their life.

NLP practices aim to help everyone realize that they hold the power within themselves to change their lives. They can look inside, figure out what's wrong, and change their perspective on any one thing. Not everyone is going to be able to do this easily, but everyone can at least try.

Since meaning is so subjective, it can be easy to alter what others think. Many people are so lost in what they actually believe that it can be easier to latch onto the ideas of others. This kind of thing is what can become manipulative and harmful. Some who follow NLP practices end up taking advantage of others because they know they can plant different ideas in their brains. They can alter the feelings of others, giving what they're masking as a "solution" to the lost individual's problem. In reality, it's all just something that's going to help the manipulator get closer to their goals.

We Can Change Our Feelings

People can change their feelings when it's convenient. This can be a manipulation tactic used to persuade and control other people. Someone could go their entire lives not caring if their sibling borrowed their clothes. Then, one day, they're mad at their sibling for something else, so they flip out when their sibling borrows their clothing. This is a small example of this tactic, but it's seen often in various relationships.

Many feelings are very hard to overcome, but there are certain people that will take things as far as they can. As we get older and our meaning changes, of course, our feelings will as well.

Not everyone will change the way they think. Some people will go their entire lives with the same feelings, but the truth is, they can be changed at any time. Humans seek comfort, just like many other animals. They don't want to change their thoughts and beliefs because they're afraid of the change that it might ignite. This can lead to very destructive behavior, as unhealthy patterns lead to a stunt in personal growth.

Some people might have an easy time changing their feelings while others find it debilitating to attempt to think in any different way. There are some people that seem as though they're changing their personal beliefs daily. Others will be incredibly stubborn in changing their minds, even if it means their decisions affect the lives of other people that think differently than them.

How People Use This Against You

Once your world is defined, it can be easy to pinpoint all the things that make your world unique. Some people will start to exploit this individuality, trying to connect with you on a personal level. For example, someone might notice that you like henna tattoos, so maybe they get one in an attempt to get closer to you. They end up only doing this because they want something from you. The manipulator is breaking into the person's individual world, disguising themselves as someone they can relate to, when really, they're just trying to distract them to get close.

People will make you rethink your choices based upon your own world. They might make you question, does this fit in with your beliefs? Are you sure you're not going against anything you believe in? These master manipulators will make you question your own morals, and when your beliefs become vulnerable, they'll swoop in and try to take advantage of that.

If someone knows that you're a religious person, they might use religion against you. They'll play on your weaknesses, knowing that as a religious person, breaking your moral code can cause great pain. They can use guilt and other manipulation tactics pertaining to the things that matter to you in order to get what they want.

Mimicking Body Language

Those using NLP tactics will often begin to mimic the body language of another person in order to feel connected to them. If a person is standing with their hand on their hip, the NLP user will do the same thing. If someone is overly confident, puffing their chest with their arms tightly crossed, the NLP user will do this same thing. They'll try to match their body with the other person to make a connection, letting them know they're someone they can trust and depend on.

They might even start talking like them, and they'll certainly give into other ideas as well. If someone is overly enthusiastic, an NLP user might feed on that enthusiasm, exerting a good mood and overall happiness as well. The opposite is true too in terms of personality. If someone seems overly pessimistic, complaining often and sharing negative views, the NLP user will try to match this, giving off the same attitude.

They might even touch the other person in order to gain some sense of connection. This can be very violating, but some people feel so thrown off by this touch that they don't even notice they're being manipulated. This can happen a lot in the workplace and even in school. Maybe a teacher or boss comes up behind a worker and places a hand on their shoulder, their way of exerting their power over the other person. In order to not create an uncomfortable situation, most people just allow the other person to touch them, giving the power to the person that did the touching in the first place.

In order to avoid this, try to do strange things you wouldn't normally do, and see if they begin to do the same thing. Find a funny trick to do with your hand, like maybe tapping the top of your head lightly. Move your eyes around rapidly and tilt your head to the side back and forth. If the person you're talking to begins to do this as well, there's a good chance they might be using NLP tactics. The same goes for anyone that touches you. If you don't want to be touched, call that person out. Ask them to not touch you nicely, and you'll be surprised to find that they'll let up. The teacher or boss that always seems to put their hand on your shoulder likely won't after the first time you ask them not to because they know it's strange behavior.

Some people actually just adopt the behaviors around them because that's part of their personality. This is a result of codependency, and not always necessarily a manipulation tactic. In order to decipher someone's true intentions, you have to look at what they might gain from the situation. If they don't seem to be taking anything from the other person, it's usually harmless behavior.

Cold Reading

Cold reading is when a person tries to convince you that they know more than they do. Mentalists, mediums, fortune tellers, and psychics will often use this technique to convince you that they are more aware of you and the information pertaining to your life than they actually do. Those that know how to cold read can quickly pick up on your body language and verbal cues to gain a quick understanding of who you are and how you work. These cold readers will use a set of guesses to figure out information, analyzing body language and other responses to figure out whether they are right are not.

For instance, a psychic might start by telling a group of people that they are speaking to someone that has passed with a name that starts with "J." Most people in the audience likely know someone that has died with a "J" name, so they will start to assume the psychic is talking about the person they know. An audience member might speak up by saying, "my uncle Joe just died,' and then the psychic will play off their body language, making small general guesses that the audience member can relate to their life.

The psychic will use verbal cues to tell if they are making the right guesses. If a participant sounds sad, they know they have hit on their emotions and can use this to their advantage. If they seem confused or distant, the psychic knows that they still need to use caution when proceeding with their readings. Anyone who states that they can talk to the dead, see the future, or make predictions and assumptions about yourself is likely highly trained in reading verbal and facial cues in order to produce a convincing cold reading.

Confusing Phrasing

Those using NLP tactics love gibberish. They'll say quick phrases or hide words in bulky sentences in order to sneak in the real meaning of what they're trying to say. This is seen most often in advertisements. Maybe there will be an overload of information. Listen to a commercial in which a medication is being advertised. The entire commercial will be about how great the medication is, the last few seconds a quick reading of the warnings and cautions that come along with taking a certain pill. The same kind of thing can be seen in different interactions with various people. Kids and teens are pretty good at this. They'll ask permission for something, starting first with the reasons why someone would say yes. Then they'll quickly mention all the reasons their parent would say no, like the fact that there won't be parents and it's a co-ed sleepover.

Someone that is using neurolinguistic programming will also be very vague with what they say. They might use quick jargon to try to distract you, or they'll be so general you really aren't sure what their actual intentions are. Think back on different political phrases that were popular. Obama simply used "Change," which could appeal to anyone. Many manipulators will use vague sayings to appease those around them. They'll say, "I'll take care of it," without offering any real explanation as to how they're going to fix the problem presented. Other manipulators might include those that leave out information that could alter perspectives, sharing only general information.

Many psychics are able to have mild success because they're so general with their information. They'll start by asking someone if they've suffered a loss. Well of course, most people have. Even if it's your grandma's old best friend's cousin's dog, everyone knows someone that's died. Certain levels of spirituality are up for debate. There are still those individuals that are able to manipulate others using general information that can be applicable to anyone's perceptions, beliefs, ideas, morals, and world.

Using Your Wants

Those who are skilled in NLP practices know what you want. That's because they have serious wants too! While everyone has their own unique and individual experiences that set them apart from other people, many of us have similar goals. Achieving fame or fortune is a big one.

Happiness is another main contender for shared wants and needs amongst a wide group of people. Manipulators practicing NLP strategies know what people want, so they use those desires to in turn get what they want.

They'll feed off your emotions, making themselves seem sacrificial in the end. Many of us want to feel important, so some seek others they can help.

Those using NLP tactics are much more dangerous than your average manipulator. They actually study how the human brain works, figuring out how to use this strange process to their advantage.

Studying human psychology is important but should only be done for the sake of exploring more about an individual. It shouldn't be used against someone, and it certainly doesn't seem healthy to mimic a person's interactions just to try to get them to buy into someone.

If you feel as though someone might be using NLP tactics, it's trickier than straight up manipulation, but the same practices should be followed to try to dismantle this deception.

Chapter 3 – Subliminal Persuasion

Subliminal persuasion is a term that's mostly found in advertisement. It's often associated with the idea of tricking someone into picking up a message without their awareness. The persuasion is done on a level that those being persuaded can't initially, or easily, pick up on.

It is yet another manipulative tactic that many people use on those around them. Subliminal persuasion isn't as invasive or harmful as other forms of manipulation, but it can still be dangerous. Of all the other forms of manipulation, this might be one of the hardest to detect as well.

The idea of subliminal persuasion is that its influences are below the detectable conscious human level. Those who are being subliminally manipulated won't be able to realize what's going on until it's far too late. In some cases of manipulation, one can recognize while it's happening. For the most part, many people can go years before they realize that they were subliminally persuaded.

The Subconscious Mind

Our subconscious mind works so much harder than our conscious one. It pretty much never shuts off and is constantly making decisions for us before we even realize what's going on. Even while we rest our conscious mind, our subconscious one is putting on various movies for us in the form of dreams. The subconscious has so much information that it has to create these delusions, daydreams, and other forms of dissociation in a way to process all that it knows.

Our brain is pretty much limitless. There might actually be a number to how many things we can know, but we haven't found it quite yet. We've only made assumptions on how far we think our brain can go. Even though we can basically pack information into our brain all day, never feeling like we know too much, most of us will just use what we have already.

Our subconscious is powerful. It consumes about 95% of our brain, yet we don't have complete control over it. Our subconscious mind could be why we develop certain fears or might make up why we have certain addictions. For every time you felt as if you didn't know why you were having a certain thought or emotion, there's a good chance your subconscious brain knew exactly why.

Your subconscious mind has been working this whole time you've been slacking off! Remember that one time you stayed up all night to get a test done? You might not have specific recollection of that night, but your subconscious does. It's what's reminding you to get your work done on time so that you don't have to endure the pain you felt the day after pulling an all-nighter ever again.

The key to most of our conscious issues lie directly in our subconscious. Why might a person think dogs are so scary? They can usually look to their subconscious mind and realize that they internalized something dark in their past to make them fearful of dogs.

We'll never be fully aware of our subconscious or the way it works, but that doesn't mean we shouldn't try. The more we can understand about the innerworkings of our brains, the better we'll be at fixing it in the long run.

Subliminal Advertising

Subliminal advertising uses our subconscious against us. They sneak certain thoughts, feelings, and emotions into the things we consume in order to buy into their products more. Some countries have even banned subliminal advertising, knowing just how dangerous this manipulation tactic can be.

Advertisers know how to get into our heads, literally. They sometimes even pay people to watch their advertisements while their brain function is monitored. This is to get an idea of how our brains work while watching advertisements. They'll track eye movement to see what part of the commercial is being studied. All this information is then used against us to specifically sell something. Advertising has broken into our brains, understanding how to sell us something better than our understanding of capitalism, and what it means to be a consumer.

Think of a chocolate commercial as an example. The advertisement might be nothing more than a picture of a peanut butter cup. You see the logo for a moment, but nothing else that tells you to buy the treat. You still get the idea of the candy bar in your head, forcing you to end up buying one next time you're at the store.

While it is most easily recognizable in advertisement tactics, there are many people that continue to use subliminal persuasion in order to get what they want.

Social Media

Social media has seemingly taken over the lives of many people. Not only do people create social media for themselves, but they make pages for their dogs as well! Social media isn't all bad, but it's agreeably inescapable.

The people that you follow on social media are likely using subliminal persuasion on you without you even realizing it. They can alter what the world sees of their life, using pictures, quotes, videos, and other small glimpses into their lives. We see more than we would see of their life in any other context, so we start to use this as our identifying factors for a specific person. Many people still keep in touch with those on social media that they haven't spoken to in a decade. Their in-person perception has faded and now all that exists is who they know them for as a social media personality.

Social media has allowed us to create our own new worlds. You get to pick and choose what other people see. You only post the good stuff if you want, or you can share the bad stuff too in an attempt to make yourself vulnerable and more relatable.

All many users see is a happy face of a baby, but they don't see that the same baby puked all over its mom and the new white rug once the camera turned off.

This manipulation makes many people feel less than themselves. They feel inadequate after comparing themselves to the people online that are living so happily. Many use this form of subliminal persuasion in order to make themselves feel better.

Altering Perspectives

This type of perspective altering is seen in ways other than just social media. There are plenty of manipulators that only give others little bits of information, using a ton of energy to cover up some big secret that they don't want everyone else to know. Everyone deserves their privacy, and not all secrets are meant to be shared. There are certain things that can really change a person's perspective, and it's not always fair to keep this from other people.

Friends and family might only tell you certain parts of their life that they want you to hear, not anything that's bad. Your sister might tell you on the phone that she's doing amazing, when really, her and her husband have been sleeping in separate beds.

Celebrities are the biggest culprits of subliminal persuasion. They go as far as having teams of makeup artists, hair stylists, wig specialists, and wardrobe coordinators to create a seemingly "effortless" look.

How You're Being Subliminally Persuaded

Whether we're comfortable admitting it or not, most people are being subliminally persuaded in one way or another. Many forms of passive aggression can also be forms of subliminal persuasion. Maybe a person's mother makes a comment about how they saw someone at the store they hadn't in a while, making a comment about their weight gain.

This could also be a subliminal message about how the mother feels about her daughter's weight. The subliminal persuasion, then, is that the daughter's perception is now altered. She might feel as though she does not meet her mother's standards of beauty and will alter her life as a result of this mild manipulation.

This is the trickiest of all the persuasion tactics discussed in the book so far.

Those that are doing the subliminal persuasion are usually so lost in their delusions that they'll never recover. They won't be the first to admit that they might carry around some manipulation tactics.

Asking for More

One method that a subliminal persuader uses is to ask for more than they actually need. Perhaps someone needs $5,000, but they know that's a big amount to ask for. So, they'll actually end up asking for $12,000, knowing that's a massive amount of money for someone to borrow. The person they asked might feel bad that they need so much money, and instead offer half in the amount of $6,000 still wanting to help even though they can't give the full amount.

The person that gives in are then under the impression that they have to give at least something. They feel bad for not having enough to give for the original offer. Really, the master manipulator knew all along that they really only needed $5,000.

The person that was subliminally persuaded might end up feeling guilty because they couldn't give more. Even though that person already asked for something once, they can come back because the person that was manipulated still didn't feel like they had given enough.

Doing Favors

Someone that might subliminally persuade another person might first ask for a favor. In some manipulation cases, a person might blatantly tell another what to do, or at least manipulate them in an attempt to get what they want. A subliminal persuader might just ask for the favor, giving the illusion that they are in need of some sort of help. The person being manipulated feels like they should help out, as they might have a need to care for others. They are also giving the illusion that they are worth doing the favor for.

Those that were subliminally persuaded then might feel as though they're special because they had the privilege of helping another person. They feel good about themselves, like they had value and were helpful to someone. Really, the manipulator just used that need to care to their advantage, getting what they wanted from the person that was manipulated.

This method is seen most amongst bosses. They'll appoint a member of their team to a special position, making them feel like a superior employee. In reality, it was a task anyone could do, and the boss just didn't want to do it themselves.

If you think you might be being subliminally persuaded, it might be a good idea to ask if the person that asked for the favor can do it themselves.

Why might they be asking you? What personal gain do they have when you specifically do the task?

Being Flattered

Flattery is great, but many people use it as a manipulation tactic. They think if they can build someone up and really make them feel good about themselves, then they'll be able to get anything they want out of them.

Children are great at flattery and learn at an early age how to trick people into doing what they want. They understand using charm can lead to happiness in other people, which will lead to them doing things for the manipulator. Most children become aware of this behavior, but many adults continue to practice this subliminal persuasion. A young woman might flatter an older man that isn't all that attractive, but maybe he has money.

This is common in abusive partners as well. They might feel as though they can build up their significant other as much as they want, only to then tear them down at a later time.

Tactically Choosing When to Ask

Those that are being subliminally persuasive will be very calculated about when to ask for something. They'll put effort into deciding when the right time to ask for a favor might be.

They'll choose a time when you might be tired, or maybe even in a really good mood. They'll wait until just the right time to ask for something in order to ensure the person that they are asking will absolutely say yes.

Someone that's subliminally persuading you will also try to only ask in public settings, thinking that they're giving you the upper hand. They'll take away the opportunity for an uncomfortable confrontation. They also might ask in front of friends and family, making the person that's being subliminally persuaded feel as though they're having an opportunity to show off how generous they are.

Conclusion

Anyone has the potential to be a manipulator, just like anyone might find themselves to be a victim of manipulation tactics. There's no set of rules that it takes to become a manipulator, and even the strongest of people might find themselves under the influence of other people's ideas. It usually starts in childhood, though there are other reasons it might develop later in life. Not all manipulators are bad, and sometimes it developed as a survival tactic.

These behaviors can be incredibly dangerous and can ruin people's lives. Some forms of manipulation can be good, like a lawyer advising their clients to accept certain plea bargains. Other forms can be very dangerous, like a holistic doctor denying a patient the right medical care even if they require it for survival.

Not everyone that is a manipulator will be ready to accept that fact. People who exhibit gaslighting tendencies might be resilient to the acceptance that they can be manipulative.

It can be a challenging truth to face, but manipulation has to be recognized in order for more growth to take place. Some people might display aggression when confronted with the idea that they're manipulators. Others might understand that they've been taking advantage of others completely and express a desire to change their behavior.

This book could be read over and over again, but nothing will change unless there is action taken now. It's up to the reader to recognize these behaviors and use their strength to work through their issues. It's not going to be easy for everyone, but it takes time and practice and should be treated with patience throughout the process.

Not every time manipulation is recognized is the time to confront the issue. Sometimes, you will have to sit with the discomfort and just recognize that the other person is trying to take advantage of you. Unless your immediate safety is threatened, don't bring up the manipulation if it's not the right time. If a manipulator is confronted in the wrong setting, it can end up making them internalize their feelings, pushing the reality further down so that they don't have to admit that they're wrong.

A person that admits they have been manipulated can become rather vulnerable. It's important to remember individual worth and value in a process that can sometimes feel so draining. A person that has been manipulated is not weak, dumb, or ignorant. Manipulators are skilled in using other people, and it's not the victim's fault they were taken advantage of.

It might be a challenging process, but it's necessary in order to achieve a higher quality of life. Everyone deserves to have their own voice, and no one should have to experience unfair manipulation.

Dark Psychology

The Practical Uses and Best Defenses of Psychological Warfare in Everyday Life

How to Detect and Defend Against Manipulation, Deception, Dark Persuasion, and Covert NLP

Introduction

Do you feel like you are merely a pawn in someone else's deceptive chess game? Are you tired of being manipulated at every turn? Would you like to be able to detect and discern genuine emotions in others, so that you can proactively protect yourself from being emotionally abused and manipulated? Then this resource is the perfect book to empower and transform you! *Dark Psychology: The Practical Uses and Best Defenses of Psychological Warfare in Everyday Life* helps you understand more than just the basics of human behavior. Instead, it takes you on an in-depth journey that explores the darker recesses of the human mind and provides insightful, practical steps on how to strengthen your mental defenses against such negativity.

Inside this book, you will learn the following skills:

- Fundamental facts about dark psychology
- How to recognize and separate truth even when it has been masked masterfully within a web of lies
- Aspects of your daily life that make you vulnerable to the manipulations of others
- A five-step program to help you break free of victimization
- How to protect yourself from the influences of dark psychology

If you or any of your loved ones have suffered emotionally, or if you are currently living through a nightmare that is directly related to the inherent dangers of dark psychology, then this book can illuminate your life! And even if you are simply curious about how dark psychology works and would like to know how to better protect yourself, this book that breaks down this complex phenomenon in the simplest terms.

Dark psychology is not a novel concept, so this book does not herald any ground-breaking discoveries. However, this topic has always been shrouded in hushed tones; there is still so much information out there that has gotten lost in barely understandable psychobabble that leaves you more perplexed than informed.

In sum, this book seeks to demystify dark psychology and equips you with the practical knowledge to protect yourself against it.

So, if you're ready, flip over to the next page and get ready to change your life.

James W. Williams

Why I wrote this book

Growing up, we lived next door to this vibrant lady who can only be described as the sweetheart of the neighborhood. It seemed like she always had a smile on her face and a kind word for everyone, whether child or adult. I cannot remember a single encounter with her that was ever in the slightest bit unpleasant. This impression of her transcended more than just my childhood impression of her. In fact, my whole neighborhood collaboratively felt the same way about her.

The only dark clouds I could see around her involved the fact that she was literally alone. She had kids, no boyfriends and not much family. She ran this tiny art and craft store that was pretty popular in the area, and I think she seemed content and happy with her role. When my Nana passed on, this inspirational woman was one of the few neighbors who brought in food every day for more than a week. From that moment on, she was more than just a friendly neighbor: she became family.

Fast forward to 2 years later, when we heard the news that she was getting married soon. My mom and her friends had tried to match her with some of the locals, but nothing worked. So, news of her imminent marriage was very welcome. We didn't know much about her suitor, only that he was fighting on the front lines and was madly in love with her. If it was possible for this sweet woman's smile to become brighter, it certainly did. I remember my mom using the expression, "walking on air" to describe this woman's perpetual mood.

A month or two to the wedding, this inspirational woman put up a for sale sign on her store and her home. She revealed how she and her fiancé were working towards making a down payment for their new home, and they wanted to make sure that everything was put in place before the wedding date. A week before the wedding the house and the store were sold. She wired the money to her fiancé and redirected her focus to finalizing the wedding preparations.

My parents invited her to spend the days leading up to the wedding in our home. It was supposed to be our family's gift to her. Two days before the wedding, her fiancé called, and we all took turns speaking with him. He had a strange accent, but we didn't give it too much thought after she explained that he had spent more than a decade in the Middle East. Apart from the accent, he generally sounded like a good guy. The next day, she tried reaching him to determine his whereabouts, but she was unable to reach him.

She started to worry, but my mom and dad reassured her and told her he was probably on a flight back to the country. She tried to find comfort in their support, but you could tell that she was worried. Every time she tried to smile, she faltered. She clung desperately to the phone: each time it rang, she jumped in fright. By the morning of the wedding, there was still no call from him. What started out as a beautiful day was beginning to look like a nightmare.

My dad kept checking the local stations for any news on a missing flight or maybe a plane crash. Mom was doing all she could to stop the tears. By the time the day was over, the wedding didn't look any different from a funeral. The only thing missing was the dead body. Overnight, this thriving and much-loved businesswoman wound up broke, homeless, and heartbroken. Her crime for the grim punishment was falling in love.

In the days following her no-show wedding, she had a psychological breakdown. She was committed to a psychiatric ward for a few months before she had to be moved to another state to live with a distant relative. I never saw her smile again after this devastation.

As a kid, it was hard to fully understand what had happened. All I heard was that she was a victim of an online scam. But her story left an impression that followed me deep into my adult years. Online scams occur on different levels, but the patterns are fundamentally, the same. The perpetrators concocted a dark and intricate web of deceit that entrapped their victims using all or most of the markers associated with dark psychology. They set the bait, and when the victim bit, they created a false sense of security. This mechanism allows them to further manipulate the victim into doing exactly what they wanted, before they made the final strike.

Despite the reports and general awareness created about online scams, many people still fall victims to crooked fraudsters every day. This scenario encouraged me to think that this type of ruthless behavior is not just indicative of online scams. We also see this coercion in our everyday lives. People in dysfunctional relationships with partners who use them in the most obvious ways, but they continue to stay in those relationships because they seem to be under some kind of spell. We see kids make friends with people who influence them in terrible ways: and despite the solid home training, they make the wrong choices repeatedly. Their parents are helpless and baffled by the power that these so-called friends have over their kids.

We tend to focus more on the terrible actions and consequences than the patterns that play out before these "crimes" occur. This failure to examine the patterns likely explains the increase in victim rates despite the widespread awareness campaigns. In turn, I wrote this book and conducted extensive research based on this reason. I also assessed studies on notorious perpetrators of these crimes, and I made a startling observation. There was one consistent factor in everything. The players changed, the technology was, the times progressed, but the game patterns are almost always the same. Plus, all of these patterns are clearly attributed to dark psychology.

So, to help you and your loved and consequently build a strong mental and emotional defense against such evil influences, this book, *Dark Psychology: The Practical Uses and Best Defenses of Psychological Warfare in Everyday Life* was born.

James W. Williams

PART ONE:

FUNDAMENTAL FACTS ABOUT DARK PSYCHOLOGY

WHAT IS DARK PSYCHOLOGY?

"It cannot be seen, cannot be felt, cannot be heard, cannot be smelt

It hides behind stars and under hills and empty holes it fills

It comes first and follows after. Ends life, kills laughter."

J.R.R Tolkien – The Hobbit

The mind is one of the most complex aspects of human nature. The workings of the mind denote something that has both puzzled and intrigued mankind for as long as we can remember. Philosophers, psychologists, and scientists have sought to unravel the mysteries of the mind. It is a generally held belief that the human mind keenly influences our behavior and actions. Thus, so much research work has gone into understanding the mental process that a person undergoes before taking an action, whether good or bad.

Some attempts at studying the human mind have concentrated efforts on the brain. These studies examine the physical aspects of the brain with a focus on how information is acquired, processed, interpreted, and stored. Essentially, scholars hope to get a better understanding of how the brain can affect a person's way of reasoning. These studies have paved the way for progress in managing debilitating conditions like Alzheimer, perception difficulties, and even memory loss.

The more familiar aspect of the study of the human mind is psychology. At some point in our lives, we have either consulted a psychologist or have likely known someone who had to consult one in order to navigate tougher emotional battles. In reality, life's experiences break us down in ways we often cannot fix on our own. Sometimes, the breakdown is as a result of certain biological markers inherited from our parents. Emotions like depression, anxiety, and fear darken our daily experiences making it difficult to thrive. With a combination of drugs and therapy, we are able to protect ourselves from the internal darkness.

But, what about the darkness in others?

Everyone has the capacity for doing great good. We also possess the ability to do great evil. Beneath emotions like sadness, depression, joy, and happiness is a deep rooted desire that can lead us to deliberately harm others if those urges are not regulated. These darker desires derive from more primitive instincts like our flight or fight response that promotes our survival. Sometimes, there is only one word that qualifies the human response to these dark emotions...evil.

Dark psychology is a study of the human condition in relation to the psychological nature of humans to prey on others. In lay terms, dark psychology explores the aspect of human nature that allows us deliberately and willfully take actions that bring harm to our fellow humans. Mind you, the use of prey in this context does not necessarily translate into the physical harming of a person, although there is a branch of dark psychology that is dedicated entirely to this. In subsequent chapters, we will touch briefly on those areas to obtain a better understanding of the topic.

In movies or books, you may have encountered words or phrases alluding to "a darkness within." Even some of the most famous philosophers made references to this. The revered book of the Christians talks about how "the heart of man is desperately wicked." We have all probably met that one individual who we have described as exceptionally calm or reserved in social settings, only for this same individual to perpetrate an act so devious that we find it difficult to associate that act with this individual in question. Sometimes, we are that individual. As surprising as it may seem, it is not entirely shocking.

Those cases are just triggered responses to external situations. The pot was stirred so to speak and those dark emotions that hid beneath simmered to the surface. Usually they recede once control is exerted. Everyone has a latent tendency to be a bit naughty or just downright evil, if the rights "buttons" are pushed. Some other individuals, on the other hand, are fully in control of these dark emotions. They nurture them, feed them, and when it serves their own purposes, they willfully unleash them at another person's expenses.

Sometimes, these emotions are groomed from an early age. A child learns that if he or she cries in a certain way, the adults in their lives rush to do their bidding. If the parents do not impress upon the child early enough the wrongness of this, the child grows up thinking people in one's lives can be manipulated into doing his or her bidding. The crying would cease to be a weapon, as the child grows, he or she may often continue in manipulative ways. While the child won't resort to tears, he or she will use emotions to blackmail victims. So, what started out as an innocent childish behavior becomes a dark need to control.

The lengths that this individual would go to exert control would define the intensity of one's actions. Dark psychology is all about studying the thought process of a person like this. It seeks to understand the motive behind these actions, the patterns exhibited from before these acts are performed, to after and offers more light on how a person can willfully see those actions to conclusion, knowing the hurt and pain it might cause to another individual. Dark psychology illuminates the dark side of human nature.

How to Analyze People, Persuasion, and Dark Psychology

THE EFFECTS AND IMPACT OF DARK PSYCHOLOGY

"When you light a candle, you also cast a shadow."

Ursula K. Le Guin

Given the little we now understand about dark psychology, we know that some of the most shocking criminal offences are rooted in certain personality traits related to dark psychology. But that realization is a broader side effect. I want to bring it closer to home, to you and me. How does this dark psychology affect us...if it even affects us at all? I can assure you that there are no "ifs" to this question, and in a few short moments we will understand how.

The effects of dark psychology are experienced by both the perpetrator and the victim. To recognize the impacts, we need to explore some elements of dark psychology. People who exhibit certain personality traits that are considered dark such as narcissism, psychopathy and Machiavellianism are prone to experiencing difficulties in all aspect of their relationships. If all three traits are present in one person, he or she has a higher propensity to commit a crime. The three personality traits mentioned have specific characteristics that are grouped under them.

Narcissism, for instance, is characterized by a sense of entitlement, feelings of superiority, deep seethed envy of the success of others and exploitative behavior. Psychopathy has an absence of guilt, lack of empathy, destructive impulsive behavior, egocentricity, and inability to accept responsibility as some of the characteristics. Selfishness, ruthlessness, and manipulative behaviors are indicators of Machiavellian traits. Separately, these traits are problematic but combined, they can spell trouble, especially in a person's relationship with others. In the workplace for instance, that person would typically act in these usual ways:

- Underperform in the office, even during the most mundane tasks
- Disrupt workflow due to the inability to get along with others
- Would be intensely disliked by others
- One's impulsivity would facilitate questionable and unethical decisions
- If put in an administrative capacity, he or she would more likely to commit white collar crime

But it is not just work relationships that suffer. In personal relationships, too, one is bound to encounter the following problems:

- The constant need for attention and validation can be exhausting for one's partner, thus resulting in faster expiration dates on relationships
- One may resort to physical and emotional blackmails in order to manipulate his or her partners

- One may tend to be either verbally, emotionally, or physically abusive with partners or children

People who enter relationships with these types pay a high emotional cost.

If you have encountered a person whose relationships are characterized by these experiences, for the sake of your sanity and general well-being, steer clear of this individual. If, on the other hand, you are the one who experiences this, seek the psychological help you need to get better. No matter how deep-rooted these problems are, you can improve your behaviors and experiences with the right form of therapy. The first step is recognizing the situation for what it is, acknowledging that you have a problem, and seeking help promptly.

For the rest of us, dealing with people who have the traits I mentioned above leaves us emotionally and mentally drained. Sometimes, the effect can be physical and in extreme cases, fatal. The sweet neighbor whose terrible experience led me on this journey to write this book lost everything physically and financially; her home, business, and finances, but her loss was much deeper and greater. We didn't have a relationship with the perpetrator of the act, but we became victims as well. Our losses were not as monumental as hers, but we experienced loss, too. For starters, we lost our sweet neighbor. She didn't die, but she never recovered from the experience. We lost our ability to trust strangers. Even our relationships with each other seemed to require an additional layer of trust to thrive.

The biggest impact of dark psychology on anyone is that it produces a strong sense of loss. We lose our valuables, we lose relationships, we lose ourselves [I will explain these premises in a bit]. For those who are extremely unfortunate, they lose their lives. All things considered; it is safe to say that the impact of this darkness is profound.

According to experts, if a person exhibits one of the dark personality traits, there is a very high tendency that the person will demonstrate the others. In general society, if the larger members of the society show these traits, it is safe to say that the crime perpetration rates in that society would be significantly high. That is not to say that people living in cities or countries with higher crimes are more criminally inclined. There are other contributing factors to consider, but the prospect cannot be entirely ruled out either.

One point that cannot be ruled out though is the ripple effect of actions directly related to or as a result of dark personality traits. There certain destructive behaviors that turn victims into predators as well, and this cycle continue well into the future until someone plucks up the courage and takes the bold step to break free. Children from abusive homes, for instance, more often than not grow up to become abusers. In some cases, in their attempt to break away from their parental mold, they find themselves trapped in equally abusive relationships, even if they are the not the abusers themselves. It is almost as if they have a very strong gravitational pull towards the violent elements that characterized their childhood homes.

For some others, becoming victims can have such a tremendous impact on their psyche that it causes something inside of them to snap. I have read that the "snapping" can be temporary. In a brief moment, they lose all control over their primitive instincts and act purely on the strongest emotion that surfaces which is usually anger. This condition is what causes some people to plead temporary insanity. But there are people who embrace the dark emotions that surface when they "snap." All sense of morality goes out the window. The aftermath of this is usually devastating.

James W. Williams

DAY TO DAY EXAMPLES OF DIFFERENT ASPECTS OF DARK PSYCHOLOGY

I am terrified of this dark thing that sleeps in me;

All day, I feel its soft feathery turnings, its malignity.

Sylvia Plath, *Ariel*

When you think of dark behavior, you may presume that it only applies to any crime that lands you on the front page of the dailies or becomes a feature-length film on the crime channel. In reality, it also includes quite a number of actions that have generally become socially acceptable even if we do not condone such behavior personally. We witness these instances in our homes, schools, offices and thanks to innovative technology, we now see it on the Internet. To help you get a clearer picture and hopefully a deeper understanding of this subject and to tell you how close to home these actions are, I am going to share some of the most sensational crimes stories and the seemingly inconsequential actions the led to a terrible end.

CASE STUDY ONE

News: Brutal Murder of a 14-year-old boy

Traits of the Perpetrator: Controlling, Abusive, Manipulative, Reclusive

Channel: Online Gaming

This case exemplified the tragic story of a young boy from a well-grounded home. He had the same privileges of any teenager in the same age and social group. He had a supportive mom and a dad who strived to provide socioemotionally and financially. His mother took all the necessary precautions a mother would to protect her boy from the invasive world of the Internet. Online gaming was just another hobby that any teenage boy would savor. As long as he didn't spend more than the appropriate time on it, his mother assumed that he should be fine.

But the perpetrator, who was only 4 years older, had sinister plans. By carefully manipulating his young and impressionable victim with lies, he manipulated the boy into visiting him at his place, where he committed the vicious crime. It was one of the most disturbing cases, especially when you consider the age of the victim and the perpetrator. However, regardless of his age, the perpetrator exhibited all the predatory traits linked to dark psychology and snuffed out life just to assert control.

CASE STUDY TWO

News: Worst Domestic Violence Case

Traits of the Perpetrator: Physically Abusive, Manipulative, Controlling

Channel: Relationship

Love indeed is a beautiful thing. When you enter into a relationship with someone, you embark with the hopes that this person will love and care for you. You vow that you will nurture and protect each other. In the modern love language, it is you and the person against the world. Indeed, it started out this way in this relationship. A single mom was working hard to care for and provide for her son when she met this charming man who was basically what she had always prayed for in a man.

He was charming, considerate, and seemed to love her boy just as much as he loved her. In order to fully make himself available for this young family, the man quit his job and devoted himself to caring for her until his true dark nature emerged. Using her love for her family, he manipulated her into isolating herself from those closest to her. He orchestrated the loss of her job, which resulted in the loss of her home. This sinister action ensured that she was entirely dependent on him. He relocated her to his own apartment, where she was constantly subjected to round the clock torture that involved some of the most inhumane treatments.

His careful manipulation of the woman as so effective that when he gave her the option of how she would like to be killed, she actually mulled the thought over because she felt she had no choice and deserved no better. Chance and an act of bravery on her part led to her rescue and incarceration of the perpetrator.

CASE STUDY THREE

News: A prominent Minister of God accused of molesting underage members

Traits of the Perpetrator: Manipulative, controlling, egocentric

Channel: Religion

There is a sacred relationship between religious leaders and their followers. The leader is meant to be the moral compass that directs the followers in the right way to lead their lives. For years, regardless of religion, leaders have abused their position of power by choosing instead to act out the biblical reference of a proverbial sheep and shepherd role. Except, instead of being shepherds, they choose to be wolves.

Having established his authenticity by claiming to have direct communication with God, this religious leader conned his members with his vision. At some point, he proclaimed himself God and claimed he had a mandate to sleep with 7 virgins who also happened to be minors. He was later charged to court and convicted of the crime.

These three cases here are sensational, but the lesson is what I want to call your attention to. These crimes were not random, spur of the moment type of crimes. They involved careful orchestration that groomed the victims and pulled them in that false state of trust and safety before they struck. As a matter of fact, the way the events played out conjures the role play between a predator and its prey. First, the victim is stalked and observed. Then based on the information obtained during the observation process, the predator makes a move. Only this move is not to strike but to charm their prey and make them feel loved and nurtured.

It is like they wear a mask and portray characteristics that they know appeal to their victims.

Gradually, trust is established. The next goal is to get their prey to depend on them. Whether it is financial dependence, emotional dependence or spiritual dependence, the outcome is the same. They want to feel needed. Then they isolate their prey, after which, they strike. It is never like those crimes that you suspect or see coming a mile away. Instead, it is like a song and dance routine that gives the predator the upper hand and leaves the victim vulnerable. In the next chapter, we will discuss just how vulnerable we are.

HOW VULNERABLE ARE WE TO DARK PSYCHOLOGY?

"To share your weakness is to make yourself vulnerable; To make yourself vulnerable is to show your strength."

Criss Jami

If we examine the case studies used to illustrate the effects of dark psychology in our everyday lives, the question of our vulnerability comes to the forefront. The channels these perpetrators used are somewhat innocent and not exactly what one would classify as a precursor to doom. So, it is safe to say that the premises on which the platforms were used expedited the dreadful final result. In the first case, you have a kid in a gaming chat room for his peers. His passion for the game brought him there, but it was his need to connect with friends that informed his decisions; finally, it was this need that the predator exploited.

In the second case study, again, it was a basic human need to connect with someone on an intimate level that was preyed on, and the victims' emotions were manipulated to alter her reality. From love, she descended into an emotional state of worthlessness, and the perpetrator inflicted further harm on her because of her vulnerable state. In the third case, the victims placed their faith in the wrong deity, even though their intentions were virtuous and very human. The predator presented himself as a vital link to what they desired to attain spiritually, and this desire became the premise for their doom.

Likewise, I have studied other cases following this same pattern. The desires and emotional needs of the victims were twisted and turned against them. This gives credence to the belief that our needs and desires are what make us vulnerable to these predators. Does this line of thought mean we should shut ourselves down emotionally? Let us give this further thought.

We have been groomed to show strength, to not give in and to never let anyone see our fears. In sum, we are been taught that going contrary to these instructions would result in people reading you as weak and vulnerable. Ironically, it is the very thing that separates us from other creatures that have also become the very source of both our strength and weakness. And that thing is our humanity. We are vulnerable simply because we are human. Our desires, our hopes, our aspirations, our quests for living transcendent lives reflect some of the things that make us vulnerable.

But the day we cease to possess any of these things, we cease to be human: and when we are no longer human, we become the thing that we are trying to protect ourselves against becoming. When we stop believing, when we stop caring, or when we stop being vulnerable, we become these seemingly soulless individuals whose sole mission is to satisfy their wanton lusts with ruthlessness regardless who would be hurt in the process. That said, while we acknowledge that our humanity makes us vulnerable, we must not forget that we can also draw strength from it.

This brings me to the biologically ingrained need for humans to connect with others. Recognize that this need is a healthy emotional human need. Without a connection with another human being, we fail to function properly. In fact, I read of a study where test subjects were isolated and studied. Short periods of isolation increased anxiety levels and affected productivity. Long periods of isolation had side effects that were worse. The subjects became depressed and found themselves brooding on dark thoughts for extended periods of time.

Specifically, the subjects' mental health was not the only factor that suffered. Physically, their sleep and eating patterns changed. They lost track of time and gradually lost their grip on reality. They started experiencing early onset paranoia. The conclusion was that we need contact with other humans to thrive. This need to connect with others makes us vulnerable because people have different agendas for establishing connections with others. Some are genuinely looking to build good relations, but others just want to use the people in their lives to obtain some other goal or objective like wealth or influence. For some others, their intentions are even more sinister. The secret to navigating this maze of human agenda is knowledge.

There was a time that the saying "ignorance is bliss" was touted in many circles as a mantra to emphasize the burden of the responsibility that comes with knowledge. I can assure you that the price you pay for ignorance if far greater than burden that knowledge brings. If you want to win this mental warfare against the enticing influences of dark psychology, you need wisdom and the right application of knowledge in what you do. Giving up on having feelings might seem like the ideal solution, but there are recorded cases where this backfired and resulted in even greater losses. Choosing to be distrustful and becoming reclusive made the victims even more vulnerable and susceptible to a vicious predatory attack.

So, instead of shutting down opportunities to build relationships with others, you should stay open but be cautious when it comes to your needs and feelings. I am also aware of cases where the victim's emotional needs overpowered his or her rational thinking. And this is what put the victim in harm's way. Our feelings can act as a navigational system that guides you to your needs, and there are certain feelings that actually act as your biological defenses against threats like the ones we have been talking about. As we explore the subject in detail, you will better understand what those feelings are; as well as how to train yourself to recognize those emotions. Until then, if you are taking anything away from this chapter, it should be the knowledge that yes, you are vulnerable. But, by acknowledging and embracing those vulnerabilities, you can transform your greatest weaknesses into your greatest strength.

PART TWO:

ANALYZING DARK PSYCHOLOGY

MANIPULATION

"Manipulation fueled with good intent can be a blessing.

But when used wickedly, it is the beginning of a magician's karmic calamity."

T. F. Hodge

In plain terms, to manipulate someone is to control or influence that person cleverly or unscrupulously. Like it or not, we have all manipulated a person or a situation for a desirable outcome. It sounds quite dark but let me lighten the mood with a story from my mischievous childhood.

As a child, I had a habit of conveniently falling sick when I didn't want to go to school. Initially, my parents would fawn over me whenever this happened. After two emergency trips to the clinic, my mother suspected my antics. The next few times after that, I wasn't taken to the clinic, but I was allowed to stay home. During one of my tummy episodes, my friends called me excitedly to inform me that a local actor was coming to the school for a visit. I ran to my mother, begging to be taken back to school forgetting that I had "an unbearable tummy ache." My mom told me she wasn't going to take any chances and advised me to remain at home. No amount of begging or pleading could change her mind, not even after I admitted to faking my stomach pains. When I got to school the next day, I was green with envy when my friends showed me all the cool things mister actor brought for them. Suffice it to say, I never faked sickness again to escape school.

This story is just one of many when it comes to the things that we do to manipulate a situation. I still know of many adults who fake a cold to get a day off work. This acting is not entirely bad is it? Sometimes, we have been manipulated into making choices that are beneficial for us. A friend gives you a nice pair of running shoes and a one-month subscription to a local gym, so you know they want you to step up in the fitness department. Ever showed up at a lunch date with a friend only for a prospective date and a sudden emergency for your friend of course) also occurs? I have been there. Interestingly, when we feel threatened, one of the techniques we employ to escape that unpleasant situation, if blunt force is not an option, is also manipulation.

That is to say, the art of manipulation is part of our nature. However, when it comes to psychological manipulation, things get darker and more sinister. In this situation a person's actions or thoughts are influenced with the use of underhanded tactics that are either abusive, deceptive or even both. In this context, the person who is being manipulated isn't given the choice to either accept or reject the will of the manipulator. He or she simply coerced into compliance.

Manipulators have their reasons for doing what they do. Sometimes, it is something as basic as getting financial gains like the fictional soldier who duped my neighbor of all her life savings. In the workplace, these people are committed to furthering their own personal agendas, even if it would mean ramming a few heads against each other. Their principle is very simple; if you want it, you have to reach out and take it. In relationships, it is usually about getting power and staying in control. The need to be in charge fuels everything they do and sometimes they can go extreme lengths to achieve this. And then you have who love to manipulate people for recreational purposes. They are just bored, and they use their manipulative games to pass time. It is crude and vicious, but this mentality reflects their thought processes.

One of the most common tactics employed by manipulators is lying. A master manipulator is skilled in the art of deception. He or she adept at coming up with grand stories that have no real bearings on the truth. Or one goes for subterfuge and lie by omission. Some people are so good at their lies that you almost never realize the lie until it is too late. Another tactic employed by manipulators is guilt tripping and shaming. When confronted for something they have done wrong, they instantly deny it and then promptly turn the tables around by making you feel bad for questioning them in the first place. To further strengthen their hold on their victim, they vilify them thus effectively turning the victim into the abuser. You would find this kind of manipulative technique in domestic cases where the abuser would claim that the victim's character, words, or actions prompted his or her own behavior in the first place.

Other subtle techniques used in manipulation include the use of evasive, non-committal responses to questions asked. Rationalizing actions, if they are caught, and spinning the reality to match their narrative is also common. Some manipulators employ sex and seduction to carry out their devious objectives. When caught with their hands in the proverbial cookie jar, anger and projection of blame are quickly used to manipulate the situation in their favor.

However, manipulators are not always random in their selection of prey. There are specific traits in their victims that attract them, and certain vulnerabilities also make it easier for the manipulator to perpetrate their crimes. Lonely people with poor self-esteem and an eagerness to please are easier to control than the assertive social type. Although, there are people who exhibit characteristics that are similar to the later who end up being manipulated as well. For such people, manipulators study their personality flaws and weaknesses before using it against them. Impressionable people are likely to be fooled by appearances. Brash individuals who tend to make compulsive decisions are more likely to be manipulated into making snap decisions that have long term impact. People who are greedy and materialistic have a higher tendency of being scammed.

James W. Williams

DECEPTION

"Just because something isn't a lie, doesn't mean that it isn't deceptive.

A liar knows that he is a liar. But one who speaks mere portions of truth in order to deceive is a craftsman of destruction."

Criss Jami

Deception is defined as the act of hiding the truth, especially to gain an advantage. This may seem like manipulation but, there is a distinct difference. Deception is often employed in the act of manipulation and is one of the many layers in a manipulator's scheme. The goal of deception is to fool and trick the other party. While manipulation is much deeper than that: it does not negate the adverse effects of deception. A lie may take a long time before it is uncovered, but when it is, the damage and destruction it leaves behind in its wake can be devastating.

I know the story of a man who had been married for over 25years. That marriage produced 3 children between the ages of 11 and 17. All was rosy for the family. The kids went to the best schools and enjoyed the luxuries of life thanks to the wealth obtained through years of hard and resilience by the man. He spoiled his children by ensuring that whatever they needed, he provided. And who could blame him? For the first 7 years of their marriage, the couple was unable to conceive. They sought the help of specialists, spiritualists, and even tried a few unorthodox practices all to no avail. At a point in the marriage when things were at an all-time low, his wife got pregnant. He was overjoyed. When the couple added two more children to the family, it felt as though life could not get any better, but it did.

His wealth grew exponentially, and the timing was perfect. One day, the couple got a call that their eldest was involved in an accident. A lifesaving operation that involved the donation of an organ was required. In the process of donating his organ to save his child, he got to uncover the terrible secret his wife had kept for many years. The child was not his. In fact, none of the children were his. Broken, hurt, and ashamed, he took his own life, but not without cutting off his wife and children from his wealth. This deception started out as a lie to one person, but at the end of the day, 5 people (including the deceiver) were affected by it. Besides, the pain experienced by the extended family, friends, and colleagues also impacted others.

In another situation, a young startup firm recruited the services of an accountant to handle their financial affairs. The owner of the startup quickly grew fond of this young accountant. It was a strictly business relationship, but there was a sense of friendship there, too. As the company grew and expanded their operations, the business owner turned most of the administrative responsibilities to the accountant. He proved competent and was entrusted with even more responsibilities. These responsibilities came with many perks and benefits. For a while, life was looking good. But when a failed transaction prompted a quick check on the company's records, the owner was unprepared for the revelation that unfolded. Over the years, he and his company had been systematically robbed to the point where the company's accounts were in the red. The accountant fled and he was left to clean up the mess. Within months, the company folded up. 43 people lost their jobs, the business owner lost all of his investment, and relinquished his ability to trust.

The crude fact about deception is that it is built on the very emotion that is essential for human relationship...trust. For an act of deception to work, a form of relationship has to be established between the deceiver and the victim. The greater the trust, the greater the betrayal. And when there is a deep betrayal, the destructive impact often goes beyond the two individuals involved.

However, deception isn't always something that is done to others. Sometimes, it encompasses the lies we tell ourselves. We justify certain actions with the deep lies we tell ourselves. Just like manipulation, lying is also something that everyone does. Some of us may have developed certain moral principles that make it difficult for us to tell blatant lies or associate with people who do so. But it doesn't stop us from telling lies albeit "little" lies. Knowing the answer to a question but choosing to deny knowledge of it in a bid to preserve one's social grace is a lie.

Let me explain: let's say you witnessed your boss toss your colleague's project [something that he or she worked really hard for] in the trash and you listened as the colleague talked extensively about how horrible he or she thought the idea was. You hum and ham and then you leave the office only to be confronted by the colleague who enquires about the boss' thoughts on the project. Telling the truth in this instance would do more harm than good. And so, you lie. Your intention to deceive your colleague was for his or her own.

In dark psychology, the intent to deceive presents more benefits to the deceiver than it does to the victim. As mentioned earlier, manipulators use deception to strengthen their hold on their victims. For deceivers, the deception gives them an opening into developing a relationship with the victim. The goal is to exploit this relationship for their benefits. One of the most recent forms of deception employed today is deceptive affection. People claiming to feel more love or emotion for you than they actually do.

There are not many things that one can use to describe the feeling of being told that someone loves you. This is especially gratifying for people who have craved this experience. The deceiver gets the benefits of declaring this false affection in the form of trust, sex, and sometimes money.

James W. Williams

HYPNOSIS

"The scientific dictator of tomorrow will set up his whispering machines,

and his subliminal projectors in schools and hospitals

(children and the sick are highly suggestible)

and in all public places where audiences can be given in a preliminary softening up of suggestibility –

increasing oratory or rituals."

Once upon a time, the idea of hypnosis was relegated to the world of make belief that a person's mind could be controlled by the swinging of an object and the snapping of fingers was considered an incredulous idea. My first encounter with hypnosis was at a magic show. The magician called a member of the audience on stage and then he put "her under." In that state, she did some weird things that I am pretty certain she would have been too mortified to do in her right senses. When he snapped her out of it, she had no idea what had transpired in the last 2 minutes. To acknowledge that someone could have that much power over you and cause you to do things you ordinarily would not do is frightful. So, I understand why we have chosen to deny it.

However, no amount of denial can change the fact that hypnosis is real and is being used much more frequently than we care to admit. In today's modern psychology, hypnotherapy has been effective in the treatment of certain skin conditions and is also used in the management of pain associated with childbirth, dental procedures and even rheumatoid arthritis. While hypnosis is certainly not your average "pat on the cheek and do as I say" type of move, certain people are more susceptible to hypnosis than others. But let's not get ahead of ourselves.

Hypnosis in psychology is described as cooperative interaction in which the participants respond to the suggestions of the hypnotist. That is to say, when a person is hypnotized, his or her actions are heavily guided by the hypnotist. In the movies, we are made to believe that a person under hypnosis becomes sleepy and disoriented. In reality, people react differently under hypnosis, but they are not as incapacitated as they appear. In fact, psychologists refer to this as a state of hyper-awareness. In this state, they experience focused attention, heightened suggestibility and vivid fantasies. People are brought into this state with the use of visualization and verbal repetition.

This tells us that not everyone can be hypnotized [clearly, you need to possess a keen ability to visualize things]. An article I read estimates the percentage of people [adults] who cannot be hypnotized at 10%. That leaves about 90% of us susceptible which is shocking considering how strongly a lot of us feel about hypnotism. I suspect that some of the negative feelings we have about hypnotism is due to wrongly held beliefs about it. Here are some of the more common misconceptions we have:

1. Hypnotism puts you under the complete control of your hypnotist.

In the movies, we are made to believe a person who is down under would have his or her actions controlled by the hypnotist. In reality, this is not true. While hypnosis relies heavily on suggestions, if your mind is not in agreement with those suggestions, you would generally reject it outrightly. So, no. You will not be crawling on all fours and mooing like a cow...not unless you want to do so.

2. You may not be able to snap out of hypnosis.

The mind is more complex than we make it out to be. The same self-protective mechanisms render it almost impossible for your hypnotists to control your actions also keep you alert and if there is any immediate danger, you can snap out of it in a moment's notice.

3. Hypnosis is some kind of dark magic or spiritual event.

Sorry to disappoint you, but this is pure science. It is based on the research work of renowned psychologists like Sigmund Freud. There is a method and process to it, and none of it requires wooden dolls and red candles. All that is needed is your consent.

4. You can be hypnotized against your will.

Again, we have Hollywood to thank for this kind of thinking. A man walks on stage, hypnotizes an entire crowd, and makes them do his bidding? Given what we now know, it's highly unlikely. As I said, they need your consent.

5. Hypnosis can enhance your abilities.

This is somewhat true and false. It depends on what you are looking at. Hypnosis can enhance your memory, but it can also give you false memories or detort that same memory as well. So, the results are really not as great as you would have hoped. It has also been linked with enhancement of performance but doesn't expect to be running the 5k marathon overnight.

Now that we have looked objectively at hypnosis or what it is, I can now tell you that at the hands of a psychopath or a person with dark intentions, hypnosis can also be dangerous. Hypnosis doesn't always involve you going into a trancelike state for it to be effective. The key elements in hypnosis are the power of suggestion and the repetitive use of words that resonates deeply with the victim. Politicians, for example, exploit this in their campaigns. They use words like change, making a difference and so on. These words trigger a deeper search within one's self and subconsciously, we find ourselves wanting that change.

You have situations where it appears a person is completely enthralled with another. After few suggestive ones from this person, the victim rushes to do his or her bidding. In books, articles and even in true life situations, you often hear or read people's description of a particular relationship as "being under a spell." This notion embodies the power of hypnosis. This hypnosis here is not referring to the kind conducted on the shrink's couch. This is more intimate, and the resultant effect can be just as devastating. Fathers have abandoned their children and given their entire wealth to a complete stranger because of this.

PROBLEMATIC BEHAVIOR

"Technological progress is like an axe in the hands of a pathological criminal."

Albert Einstein

The subject of criminal behavior is not our focus for this book, but it cannot be neglected because it constitutes an aspect of dark psychology. Profilers, criminologists, and law enforcement agencies benefit immensely from the study of criminal behavior. In psychology, the term criminal behavior is not often thrown around because the general consensus is that crime is a behavior. However, crime engagement does not necessarily make one a criminal. Of course, there is extensive debate on this type of thinking, but we should leave that for the experts. Our focus here is on the elements that make a person commit a crime.

Specifically, I want us to explore why people employ the use of dark psychology to hurt others. This hurt could be physical or emotional.

But before we go further into this, I call your attention to something important here.

Certain people do things simply because they can. Not because they were propelled by some childhood hurt, a need to perform vengeance for an offence you may ,or may not have committed. They do it simply because they can. As humans, it is in our nature to try and understand why. We want to make sense of our situation rather than believe that we are just victims of random acts. But we must also be prepared to accept that sometimes, the situation is really just as it appears: a person driven by one's own personal desire to hurt others. If you bought this book seeking to find answers to questions like that, you should also open up yourself to the possibility that this person was just downright evil.

For a person to commit a certain type of offence, there are usually certain displayed characteristics that signify this person's capability of evil. This premise goes beyond judging a book by its cover because prolific criminals are often master of disguises. They charm you right before they disarm you. In our everyday lives, these people mask themselves as one of us by pretending to have your best interests at heart. Given what we now know about manipulation, deception and hypnosis, we are aware that predators are not always strangers. So, how can you spot those things to help you make better choices in relating with people? Within this chapter, I will address 4 traits. As we delve in deeper, we will explore these traits more thoroughly.

1. Family and Friends

You know that saying, show me your friends, and I would tell you who you are? Apart from yourself, examine this person's circles. Does he or she come from a close-knit family? What is one's relationship with his or her family like? Have you met any of one's friends? If this person has no friends at all, it could be a red flag.

2. History

We like the idea of a person being completely reformed and, in all honesty, this happens. However, you shouldn't ignore the fact that a person with a bad history has a higher tendency of becoming a repeat offender. If the person was abusive in a previous relationship, there is a possibility that he or she would be the same way with you, unless the person completed or is actively undergoing treatment

3. Problems with control

People who do not have the ability to control themselves in situations that provoke them have a propensity to inflict harm on others. In the same way, people who have a problem relinquishing control can snap and lash out at the nearest victim when they lose it, and that target could be you.

4. Anti-social values

In social settings, monitor their interactions with others. People who are generally disliked by all are typically red flags. They don't have to be liked by all, but if the person is generally obnoxious, rude, and poor at getting along with people, you may have a problem on your hands.

5. Substance abuse

Dependency on any form of drug or alcohol is a clear indicator that this person is struggling with certain issues. The abuse of substance negates one's ability to reason properly and make sound decisions. A person who abuses drugs or alcohol may not be in a position to treat your relationship as a priority in one's lives. And unless this person has a way of supporting that lifestyle, you may end up paying for it directly or indirectly, which can lead to years of abuse and neglect.

These are just pointers to criminal elements in the people we relate with. As with all things human, there are exceptions and there are variables. But the biggest mistake you can make is to see definite pointers and then just rationalize them. We have a tendency to make excuses for others. The first thing we are quick to tell ourselves is that no one is perfect. But that ideology can quickly land us in hot waters. Educate yourself, be aware, and then make informed decisions. These do not guarantee that you would be able to keep these types from hurting and taking advantage of you. But you are able to protect yourself from them 100% better than if you are acting from a place of ignorance.

Some of us are inherently wired to want to fix the people in our lives. We see someone who is obviously broken and think if we love them hard enough, we can bring him or her back from the brink of whatever precipice they are on and begin our journey to a happily ever after. From my personal experiences as well as the shared experience of others, I can confidently tell you that this is highly unlikely to work. The best-case scenario is that you become broken and spend a better part of your life healing from what you could have easily walked away from earlier.

REVERSE PSYCHOLOGY

"Sometimes, I push you away

...because I secretly hope that you would pull me closer."

Unknown

Reverse psychology is a more refined form of manipulation. Technically, it is defined as a technique involving the assertion of a belief or behavior that is opposite to the one desired with the expectation that this approach would encourage the subject of the persuasion to do what is actually desired. The major difference between reverse psychology and manipulation is that the person who is being manipulated is given an illusion of choice. He or she is made to believe that one is actually making a free choice, but in reality, he or she has been subtly coerced into doing exactly what the manipulator wants. It's enlightening when you think about the thought process that goes into pulling this off until you find yourself in the same shoes as the victim.

Reverse psychology is a technique usually employed by parents in raising their children. It works well on kids who are considered "resistant" to authority. On the surface, this appears innocent with no obvious harm to the child or their psyche, but it has also been known to backfire. In our day to day activities, we use reverse psychology in our relations with others, and it is not always born from malicious intent. Let me give an example using a wedding planner and his client.

Say this client is adamant on the choices of color to use for the wedding day. There is nothing wrong with that, except that the colors in question come across as complete garish and outlandish especially when compared with the exotic venue for the wedding and the prestigious guests invited. Obviously, the wedding planner cannot tell the client one's color choices are too trashy. Instead what he does is agree with the client and then politely convey a story that hints of a very important guest [who has also been invited for this wedding] who trashed a previous event because of a similar color, but then quickly adds that he is sure they can pull it off somehow. This gives the client and pause. The client then rethinks the choices and voila, the planner gets what he wants in the first place.

Marketers employ this technique in selling their products to consumers as well. They agree with their consumer market on certain decisions and in acknowledging their agreement, so they are able to convince their customers to buy their services. But parents and business owners are not the only ones guilty of using reverse psychology. We use this technique in dating as well. Most relationship experts would tell you that we are conditioned to want what we can't have. So, to make a person like you more or want you more, you make yourself unavailable to this person. It is a paradox really. As with every form of reverse psychology, it can also backfire. Playing hard to get can appeal to the human hunting instincts but unless you plan on being elusive forever, you are going to have to stop "running." When you stop, the hunter recedes, and then you have a stalemate.

PART THREE

KEY AREAS IN OUR LIVES THAT MAKE US VULNERABLE TO DARK PSYCHOLOGY

James W. Williams

LOVE AND RELATIONSHIPS

Those that go searching for love only manifest their own lovelessness.

And the loveless never find love.

Only the loving find love.

And they never have to seek for it.

D. H. Lawrence

Now that we have gotten the gruesome part of dark psychology out of the way, let us bring things closer to home. Because, let's face it. You've read all that and probably thought to yourself, hey, this advice does not apply to me; I can never be in that situation. Granted, the chances of things getting that gruesome are rather slim. But never make the mistake of assuming you are immune to the powers of dark psychology. Its influence is much closer to you than you think. The most common place where elements of dark psychology manifest is in our love relationships with our significant other.

Love is a universal language. It is a primordial emotion that we all instinctively crave. As humans, we are designed for love. We want to love and feel loved. No one is as happy as a man or a woman who is in love and feel loved in return. Some people mate for procreation purposes. Some people mate in order to negate societal pressure. Some even mate to promote the alliance between powerful families. But, the primary reason for relationships aka getting a mate is love.

In essence, it is easy for things to degrade to a point where love is used as a bargaining chip for more power over another individual. And this is where elements of dark psychology come to play.

You have heard of the saying, "use what you have to get what you want." In the business world, that type of thinking comes with the terrain. But in relationships, it is called manipulation. Let's explore this example. A woman knows that her partner finds her sexually alluring and irresistible. Perhaps there has been something she wanted from him for a long time but has failed to obtain his willingness to comply, despite their long, drawn out conversations about it. Let's say that what she has always wanted from him is his physical contribution in doing the house chores.

His obstinate stance prompts her to device a way to make her partner become compliant. She has to do this without coming to him outright and saying something like "vacuum the living room or else there will be no sex tonight." Although that has been known to happen in certain homes, it would surely backfire, especially if you are dealing with people who have a natural dislike for taking instructions from others no matter how well it is phrased. So instead, she bids her time. When she finds him in the middle of doing a random chore, she pounces on him. Giving him sweet accolades and uttering things like how she finds him so [emphasis on the "s"] attractive when he is doing [whatever it is she finds him doing] and then she indulges his sexual craving for her.

The impact of this tactic is even greater if he normally has to "work" to get her this excited. If she does this consistently, he subconsciously gets the message that doing home chores could reward him with having good sex later. Over time, he becomes programmed to doing the chores he would naturally have declined to do because of the sexual motivation his partner offers.

This scenario is seemingly harmless. But if you observe closely, dark psychology was used here. The fella was manipulated into doing things albeit willingly for his partner just for sex. She understood his weakness and played it to her strength to get what she wanted. The good thing is that in this case, everyone goes away happy. Because the woman gets the valuable contribution she needs from her partner and the man gets the sex he craves with the woman he craves. But things are not always this mutually beneficial when dark psychology is involved. This can get really dark for the victim. Let us look at another couple.

I would call this new couple Dave and Maya. Dave and Maya have very contrasting personalities. Dave is a home buddy, and Maya is a vivacious extrovert with lots of friends. On the surface, it would seem that their difference in personalities complimented each other perfectly. This was until Dave felt the need to exert more control over Maya. But he knows (probably because he has already tried) that he can't use outright force to get what he wants. So, he begins a campaign to get Maya under his thumb. He starts by nitpicking little details about her like her choice in clothing, makeup, hair, and even makes snide comments about her weight under the guise of love, of course.

This starts affecting her confidence and when she brings up her friends, he uses flimsy incidents to illustrate and back up his theory about some fictional feud between them [things like they are jealous of you usually works]. These little seeds of doubts grow and fully blossom into a wedge that drives Maya and her friends further apart. With no friends and poor esteem issues thanks to her new-found low confidence, she is made to feel like Dave is the only person who truly cares about her and accepts her for who she is. This drives her to want to do everything she can to please Dave thus putting her exactly where he wants her to be...under his thumb and fully under his control.

In the two cases I used as an illustration, we see instances where relationships that are supposed to be about the two persons involved becomes a channel to fulfill the desires of one partner through manipulation and deception. Both relationships started out with good intentions; a while the end result of the former proved to be a satisfactory situation for both parties, the reverse is the case in the latter. The similarities here are that all victims did what they did out of their feelings for their partners. It therefore goes on to say that our desires to be loved can leave us vulnerable. Love can be manipulated and exploited for others' gains.

James W. Williams

BLIND FAITH AND RELIGIOUS BELIEFS

"If we seek solace in the prisons of the distant past
Security in human systems we're told will always, always last
Emotions are the sail and blind faith is the mast
Without the breath of real freedom we're getting nowhere fast."

Sting

I am just going to throw this out there and say that blind faith does not only refer to the belief in one supreme God or higher deity. Some people chose to believe in science. Regardless of what faith you practice, there is a fact that our faith sometimes creates a blind spot that distorts the reality causing us to make decisions that we probably wouldn't if we were in our right and proper state of mind. But before we get into the what, let us look at the why.

When I talked about vulnerability in an earlier chapter, I mentioned that the very things that makes us human are some of the things that makes us vulnerable and susceptible to the machinations of dark psychology. For some people, these influences are evident than others. Our beliefs in deities predate even the earliest civilization. Man has always regarded his existence as a small fraction in the universal scheme of things, so we believe that there are forces that are bigger, greater and divine. If you examined things logically, this kind of thinking made sense because it helped our minds cope with the inexplicable actions that happen all around us.

You see a beautiful flower and marvel at how something so exquisite and delicate could just be...without thought, without pattern, it just is. We look at the big expanse of the sky and wonder what lies beyond. Does it just go on forever? Or does it just tapper off into an endless end? When you hear the powerful roar of the waterfall or the earth-shaking sounds made by a thunder blast, even with the advancements and knowledge made available to us, we still quake in fear and awe. Back then, your choices were to either let the fear drive you insane or you rationalize the situation by pinning it on a sovereign being that is bigger than you. Some of the braver folk chose to use science to validate their explanation.

Staying with this same line of thinking, when someone we love dies, we are forced to confront our own mortality. Our grief is compounded by questions regarding life and death. Does the journey end here or does it continue into the afterlife? This has been a strong motivational force behind today's belief systems. The fear and consideration given to the life after this life has spurred many into making the "right choices" here, so that when death comes, the life that we hope continues after us is favorable for us. It is our own way of manipulating the final outcome so to speak because the alternative as it is been portrayed to us is so grim. Some people prey on our fear of the afterlife, so they use it to manipulate us into getting what they want.

If we hold this afterlife theory in such high esteem, you can imagine how we treat people who are considered mouthpieces of the deities that control the afterlife. Pastors, Imams, Rabbis, and all other form of religious leaders are held in such high reverence that their words are considered the words of the deity in question. Generally speaking, these religious leaders are meant to apply morally sound principles in accordance with their respective offices and act in the best interest of their members. If not for any other reason, at least to promote the tenets of the faith they claim to represent. However, this is not always the case as we have come to realize. A lot of religious leaders abuse their roles and influence by deceiving their members into making decisions that only serve their selfish agendas.

The common tactic is to use the name of the principal deity to twists the words that are drawn from the religion's sacred manual to mean new things that corroborate whatever story they are making up in order to help them successfully manipulate the people. A lot of people have been swindled, physically hurt and even made to commit atrocious crimes under this guise. Another method these false leaders use is claiming to have a vision or spiritual insight into a specific need that the victim has. They create an elaborate story that is a mishmash of lies interspersed with the truth (usually obtained unknowingly from the victim or third parties) and the main goal is to extort the victim for money, favor or just power play. Some victims are coerced to part with more money than they can ever hope to have. In some cases, young impressionable victims are brainwashed into living in fear under occult-like situations.

But, scenarios like these don't just end in religious houses. There are people who are not affiliated with any religion, but they like to consider themselves spiritually open. Such people would encounter fake psychics and mediums who claim to have a strong connection with the netherworld. Again, our attachment to people who have died, as well as our concerns for what happens after death, clouds our judgments and leaves us open to crooks who would like to manipulate the situation to their advantage. They employ the same trick of the false religious leaders using deception and lies to manipulate their victims. Victims go for a 10-minute psychic reading of their horoscopes and palms only to get strung along for years with promises, altered realities, and false hopes, which cause them to spend thousands and thousands of dollars searching for the elusive "truth."

People who place their hope in science are not immune to manipulations. If you are thinking that because your faith is anchored to legible and factual science, you cannot be influenced, think again. When there is a crisis, people revert to what they believe in. For a science believer, you naturally turn to science. There are cases where people with debilitating medical condition seek out unconventional medicine in a bid to outlive the disease. Knowing that the best of conventional medicine has failed, they turn to these outliers who claim to have the solution with their experimental drugs and never-been-done-before medical procedures. Unfortunately, these procedures are too risky, too expensive, and often uninsured. But the slim chance of life is worth every penny and this is what the fraudulent people exploit.

And it is not just in crisis. You have people come up with wonder solutions to a mass problem like weight loss and so on. They claim that their latest diet fad, wonder pill or technology can transform us using scientific theories that have not been tested and verified. Many people buy into the promise of this transformation based on information that has been specifically manipulated to extort victims. The main difference between religious con leaders and these purveyors of fake science is that instead of a deity, they use science when swindling their victims. And sadly, most people don't realize until is too late just how badly they are being affected.

When it comes to belief, those who use dark psychology key into your deepest needs and exploit it. They use that which you hold sacred to manipulate your thought process. And sometimes, the sacredness of it doesn't really matter. As long as it is important to you, they consider it a gold mine of some sort. And there is no greater time to mine and individual so to speak than when that individual is experiencing a crisis. This is because, in your moment of crisis, you are at your weakest and most susceptible to the influences of others and people have been known to manipulate things to their own advantage.

SOCIAL CONDITIONING

Where justice is denied, where poverty is enforced Where ignorance prevails and where any one class is made to feel that the society is an organized conspiracy to oppress, rob and degrade them, neither persons nor property will be safe.

Frederick Douglas

During a group discussion when I was in school, I heard an argument where someone vehemently declared that we are a product of our society. I wanted to dispute that right there because I was privileged to know many successful individuals who defied their society and distinguished themselves by accomplishing very impressive feats. As I grew older and experienced more of life, it dawned on me that these individuals were the "exceptions." It is an undeniable fact that the society we live in plays a tremendous role that shapes us in more ways than we can imagine. The ugly truth is that the way we think, live, and function can be traced to the influences of our society and these are some of the things that dark psychology exploits.

Social conditioning refers to the impact the society has on your life as a whole. While social conditioning looks more at your social status in terms of income, living conditions and so on, its reach can go deeper than that. Your society can and does influence your beliefs and religion. You may not be a direct practitioner of those beliefs, but you are indirectly affected by it. In certain cultures, certain days are considered sacred. That means, conducting business on those days might be considered an offence. But seeing as we have just discussed religion in the previous chapter, let us look at other aspects of social conditioning that can easily be influenced by dark psychology.

There is a general misconception that being part of a society that is more advanced makes you impervious to the influences of culture. I totally get that kind of reasoning. How can a society that gave birth to the likes of Albert Einstein and Neil Armstrong be impacted by something as ridiculous as culture right? Well, you are wrong on that count. If anything, you are even more vulnerable, and I will tell you about it in a bit.

The biggest advancement our society has made today is in the area of technology. We live in a world where things are done in a flash. Money transactions are completed at the push of a button. A businessman can conclude a deal in China, motivate his team in South America, talk his partner through a crisis at home, and deliver an impressive marketing pitch in Dubai all before the morning is done just by pressing a few buttons. This is the world we live in today. If you are coming up with a business plan in this era, your products and services have to match the same speed that we are all used or else you are setting up yourself to fail. And this is very good. Because I am fairly certain that no one misses the good old days when it took one whole month to get a mail from across the country or three puffs of black smoke shooting in the sky to tell you that your beloved loves you back. No. We appreciate the pace with which things are done these days.

Unfortunately, this speed that characterizes our daily lives makes us vulnerable to get rich quick schemes. We hear all these amazing stories of people who became millionaires overnight and on some subconscious level, we desire the same thing. Some people have exploited these desires to their advantage with what we now know as Ponzi schemes. Named after the infamous Charles Ponzi, a Ponzi scheme is a diabolical way of carrying out daytime robbery with full consent from the victim. The scam artists come up with a fictitious enterprise that promises huge returns on investment. After the victim makes an initial commitment, he is rewarded with "returns," which draw in him further into the trap the perpetrators have laid out causing him to put in more funds. To even maximize his profits, the victim is manipulated into bringing in more friends to make investments. The more friends he brings, the higher his returns. This builds a pyramid of investors all pouring their funds into this enterprise that does not exist. In reality, what the scammers are doing is simply robbing Peter to pay Paul. Then they pay themselves as well. This continues until one day; the company just vanishes into thin air leaving lots of victims stranded and without their initial investment or returns on it.

The only logical explanation we can give for a situation like this where a company with barely any registered documentation of its existence comes in and swindles hard working people who are usually smart in their dealings is social conditioning. It happened in the 1800s, in the 1900s, and it is still occurring to this very day. And despite the knowledge of its existence, people are still falling for Ponzi schemes. It is like we are just programmed to do it. Plus, it is not just a restricted to a certain class of people. Both rich people and poor people fall for it. That tells us that the perpetrator preys on something that these two classes of people have in common: is a desire to make more money and to make that money fast.

But it doesn't just end there. To successfully commit this crime, they rely on our sense of community. You are more likely to patronize the services or products of a company if you were given a direct referral by someone you trust that the recommendations of a random stranger. If your sister shows up saying she made xyz amount of money on an investment and she shows you proof of it, instinctively, your trust causes you to base your decision almost entirely on their reference. And when you get your own payout, you automatically become an ambassador for the brand. This makes you spread your own news to other people in your network and the chain continues. This is a very human behavior and a lot of manipulators would capitalize on this. As soon as they get what they need, they disappear or get consumed by their greed and get caught.

You might argue that this scenario is not likely to happen to you because you are just too smart for this, so let me bring it closer to home using technology that we go to bed with and wake up to every day. Social media is the craze of our time. People have become "overnight" sensations thanks to social media platforms like YouTube, Instagram, Twitter, and Facebook among others. This has caused some of us to nurse similar dreams, but until that happens, we are willing to settle for the likes and comments we get. The problem is that our natural desire to connect with people can become somewhat obsessive if the focus is on our virtual relationships on social media. This grows into a disturbing thought process where one's sense of accomplishment is equated with the number of likes, follows, and comments one can get from a post.

Individuals who start thinking in this manner stop paying attention to their actual real-life relationships. Instead, they lead fake and pretentious lives just so that they can get approval that in a sad way validates their daily lives. In their quest for relevance, they starve themselves emotionally and subject themselves to the sometimes cruel and disapproving opinions of others. This sort of behavior has been linked to the increase of suicidal behavior in people who use social media. It is quite ironic that social media, which was designed to help us connect with other people and build our network has broken many people instead due to its dark influences.

James W. Williams

AMBITION AND PERSONAL ASPIRATIONS

Great ambition is the passion of a great character.

Those endowed with it may perform very good or very bad acts.

All depends on the principles which guide them.

Napoleon Bonaparte

We all have a to-do list. Sometimes, this list is just a group of tasks designed to help us get through the day. And sometimes, it is a roadmap to where we would like to be in the nearest future. For example,, your grocery shopping list gets you through the day in that you are able to get what you need to make dinner and possibly the basic essentials that helps you become a better member of the society (ye olde regular bathing soap keeps the bad odors away and the society thanks you for it). But, drawing up a business plan for your startup? That is a different ball game entirely. You are trying to set yourself up for the future financially and quite possibly, providing a product or service that impacts the lives of people positively. In today's terminology, we call that "boss moves."

Ambition is what drives you towards those goals you set for yourself. You want something? You push yourself to attain it and for the more ambitious folks, when they achieve their goals, they simply push themselves some more. Ambition is an attractive trait in any human. The aspiration to be better than who, what and where you are now often puts you at the wheel that steers your life. Nobody wants to be with people who are content to sit on the couch all day doing nothing more than eating potato chips and flipping through channels. People want to be with someone who is truly excited about the beautiful future envisioned and are meticulously working to achieve it.

However, as attractive as ambition is, when it is put in overdrive, it can attract the wrong sort of people into your life because it leaves you open and vulnerable. This may sound like a contradictive statement because ambitious people are described as anything but vulnerable. But, as you will come to learn in this book, what you allow to consume you gains control over you and when you have no control, you become vulnerable. In earlier chapters, I talked about how predators use the weaknesses of their victims against them. Bearing this in mind, you would agree that ambition is an admirable trait in a person. As a strength, it can help you navigate your path to success. But as a weakness, it can very easily be the architect of your destruction.

Where ambition drives your goals, your personal aspirations, on the other hand, can be looked as your success indicators. There many similarities between aspirations and ambitions, but the main difference is the magnitude and intensity of the later. Your ambition could be to climb up the managerial ladder before the year is over, and your aspiration could be to be open up more employment opportunities when you attain that position. Ambition is more concrete in its desires while aspirations are those noble notions that we nurse to make us feel better about ourselves. On their own, neither ambition nor aspirations should bring you harm, but when other elements come into play, they can be used to manipulate and deceive you.

Most organizations believe that ambition is one of the most desirable qualities in a potential employee. Yet this is usually because ambitious people are more willing to do what needs to be done to advance the company than their more seemingly docile counterparts. People like these are very focused and have a one-track mind when it comes to carrying out their responsibilities; sometimes giving no thought to what it would take to do it even if it would mean stepping on the toes of a few colleagues. In certain contexts, this can be good. After all, the workplace and the world in general is not a playground where the rules of equity for all applies. But this attitude can quickly create a hostile work environment that makes it difficult for employees to thrive. The goals of the organization may be met consistently, but at the detriment of its employees. But this is not the immediate danger although, that is not saying that a situation like this is not an issue for concern either.

A person who does not reign in one's ambition can be persuaded and manipulated into doing things that are morally and ethically wrong just to meet his or her goals. People with lofty ambitions and aspirations that are more likely to fall for manipulative techniques that involve blackmail. For instance, a young career man with a sterling reputation and a good position within a company is more likely to do anything to retain that status quo if he is ambitious. Even if those things he is expected to do would further taint his reputation if the knowledge of those deeds ever came to light. This is not to say that the rest of us are less likely to become victims of blackmail and other forms of manipulation.

Manipulation is not about physically wielding a big dangerous axe over a person to force him or her to do something out of the ordinary. It is a game of subterfuge and deception. The manipulator acts like a mirror that captures the desires, ambitions and aspirations of the victim and then threatens the actualization of that vision by also displaying the victim's weakness. The victim is made to falsely believe that one's only hope of salvaging their dreams is to comply with the wishes of the manipulator. The stronger the ambition, the more likely the victim will comply, especially if he or she is convinced that the person can get away with doing it.

The acts they could be manipulated into carrying could be anything from undermining the authority figure in their lives, committing an act that might be offensive or one of any of whatever else the manipulator may have in mind. Let me scale this back to relatable proportions. In all of our relationships with people, there is a measure of trust. No matter how paranoid you may be, even the business relationship you have with your tailor is an indication of some level of trust in that you are trusting in someone to help you cover your nakedness without getting harmed in the process. But in as much as there is trust, there is also distrust. We strive to work through these feelings in the hope of maintaining the bond/bridge between the people involved.

At best, we aspire to maintain civility with those around us. A predator with malicious intent can expound on the distrust by sowing seeds of discord to enable him or her to get the desired results, t which could be your loyalty or that of your counterpart or sometimes even both. Little incidents are blown out of proportions and tensions are escalated in the process. Eventually, the relationship is broken down beyond repair. You on one end are hurt by the accusations, and your peer is hurt by the counter accusations. Neither of you realizing that a third party took advantage of the emotional aspirations for each other (and yes, there is such a thing) and manipulated you into the current state you are in.

This goes on to say that our aspirations and ambitions are not always about the material things that we want. It is also reflected in our perceptions and expectations from the relationships in our lives. Dark psychology is employed by the predators among us to alter this perception and manipulate it to their own advantage.

EMOTIONAL SCARS

> *It has been said, "time heals all wounds".*
>
> *I do not agree. The wounds remain.*
>
> *In time, the mind, protecting its sanity covers them*
>
> *with scar tissue and the pain lessens*
>
> *But it is never gone.*
>
> ***Rose Fitzgerald Kennedy***

One of the largest residual effects of every experience we have is emotions. They say that in life, experience is the best teacher. Having spent more than a decade trying to understand human nature, I am inclined to agree. Let me share one of my most memorable experiences from travels in recent times. I think it best illustrates the point I am trying to make. Every year, I pack up my bags and travel to explore places that are not really hot spots for tourists, but they are exotic all the same. On this particular trip, I was travelling with a tribe of natives on their annual pilgrimage journey to pay homage to a particular deity. I was not a worshipper, but they were kind enough to let me travel in their company and observe their routines. At night, as we sat by the campfire enjoying the warm glow in the dark after a nice meal, I listened to them chatter in a language I didn't understand.

My translator occasionally chimed in when there was a general laughter or question directed specifically at me. But for most part, I just observed. And that was when I saw this child, not more than 8 or 9 months, I think. I can't really tell at that age. Only that the child was crawling towards the fire. I looked around the fire, but no one seemed to be paying any attention. So, I made a move to intercept the child, but I was immediately reprimanded. All the interpreter told me was that the child was about to learn a valuable lesson, and I was concerned. The fire pit wasn't blazing hot, but some of the wood still had fire on them and there were embers lying about that was still glowing. I watched keenly.

The child, fascinated by the little flames, crawled closer and then stopped. Perhaps the heat from the fire had given him a pause. But then the brave lad decided to brave the heat and proceed. He paused at a safe distance and then held out his hand toward the flame which he promptly withdrew. His face registered a shocked expression, and I could see his lower lip quivering. I wanted to go to him but the man beside me must have sensed my intentions because he signaled me to wait. The poor baby's expression shifted from hurt to one of confusion. It was like he was telepathically speaking to the flame and asking why it hurt. He tried using his hand again, and this time he cried. The men cheered and laughed. A woman, quite possibly his mother, who must have been standing very close by quickly swooped in and carried him away.

I was incensed. I asked the translator the purpose of this. The chief responded through the translator with words that I still remember to this day. He said, it is hard to look at fire from a distance and argue against the eyes that such a glorious thing could also be deadly. Sometimes, one's hand must do the convincing when eyes fail. It is called experience. He went on to assure me that no one would have let anything dangerous happen to the child, but I get the feeling that his definition of dangerous is way different from what I imagine it to be. Now, before we veer off in righteous indignation (and rightly so) over cultural childcare practices, we should not neglect the stark truth in his words. There are lessons in life only experience can teach you, and each experience leaves an emotional scar.

There are certain experiences in life that would promptly induce the never again reaction from us. Those experiences are so deeply etched on our minds that we immediately interpret certain signs as a precursor to the event that scared us in the first place. And the second we observe these signs; our fight or flight instincts kick especially if those experiences pose a threat to us. This predictable pattern of behavior is meant to protect us in times of perceived danger. Think of it as a biological defense against what might cause us harm, or that emergency drill your body undergoes your brain senses you are in danger. What I have described here is the body's reaction to fear, but fear is not the only emotion that can be triggered by your experiences. There is a long spectrum of emotions, ranging from anger to zealousness, that can be triggered by an experience.

A woman in love memorizes her lover's scent. And every time she gets a whiff of that scent, her mood is transformed. Sometimes, it induces joy and on certain occasions, it can trigger lust. If that relationship packs up, the scents could induce sadness or rage depending on how bad the break up was. All I am saying is that emotions are part of the human experience. When we feel a certain way, we act a certain way. Certain events can trigger emotions that cause us to react abnormally. My near drowning experience as a teenager causes me to panic every time, I close my eyes under a shower. These reactions are triggered by the emotional scars we carry. Now, let me explain the science of this. When an event occurs, whether good or bad, your brain identifies that incident with a specific emotion. This would explain why something as simple as the smell of freshly baked bread can transport you to your childhood (if this was your experience).

Numerous marketing companies and advertising agencies employ this knowledge in their advertising strategy. They try to identify their product with things, experiences, or events they know appeal to you or other people like you (their target demography). Subconsciously, your brain correlates those activities or experiences with their products or services. To sell a barbecue grill, they don't come and say, "Hey, here is our awesome barbecue grill. Buy it." Instead, they feed you with images of a fun 4th of July family backyard cookout. You typically see kids running around happily, smiling grandparents chatting up some family member and the teenagers doing something cool. All of these interspersed with a nice beef cut simmering on the grill. It is almost as if they are saying if you buy this grill, you also buy into this experience. In other words, you were visually manipulated into making a purchase.

This is not necessarily sinister per se. But the regular people we meet in our everyday lives can prey on this weakness. If you are easily emotionally triggered, you can be manipulated into making rash decisions on anything from impulse purchase to falling for people on emotional principle alone. People can disguise themselves and make themselves into something they are not. They wear clothes and perfumes that make it seem as though they are wealthy and because you have a strong emotional connection with wealth, you look past other warning signs and make a regretful decision. Whether good or bad, your emotional scars can make you vulnerable to deception and manipulation.

James W. Williams

PART FOUR:
RECOGNIZING AND IDENTIFYING YOUR REALITY

ACKNOWLEDGING THE LIES WE TELL OURSELVES

Above all, don't lie to yourself.

The man who lies to himself and listens to his own lie comes to the point that he cannot distinguish the truth within him, or around him and so loses all respect for himself and others.

And having no respect, he ceases to love.

Fyodor Dostoevsky

There are so many forms of lies we hear every day. Sometimes, the lies are told to protect you from something. It could be something as trivial as keeping the knowledge of something you are not ready to know; for example, a surprise birthday party. Sometimes, the lies are more complicated but not told entirely out of malice like the telling a person about their cheating spouse. The point is, for good for or bad, we all tell lies, but no lie is more grievous than the lies we tell ourselves. There is more danger from the lies we tell ourselves than the lies that other people tell us (this would be discussed extensively in the next chapter) and here is why.

In the previous chapter, I talked about the body's biological defense when the brain senses danger or situations that threaten us. These impulses, however irrational, may seem meant to protect us. Lying to yourself deadens those instincts and opens us to possible dangers. It is like seeing a speeding car coming down the highway and making up your mind to run across the road anyway. Instinctively, your body knows that this situation is precarious. A slight miscalculation could result in a fatal accident. But instead of waiting for the car to pass, you convince yourself that you are faster than the car or that the car is farther away than it looks, or it is not speeding as fast as it appears to be. These are the kind of lies we tell ourselves.

Self-deception occurs in many forms. But the most popular form of self-deception is denial. We convince ourselves that the threat is not real or imminent, so we make risky choices that we quickly come to regret. Denial is not always a clear-cut case of admitting that something does or does not exist. Sometimes, it is masked as optimism in the face of a very dire situation. And in some cases, the very opposite happens. You are in a good situation but choose to be pessimistic and deny the possibilities. According to a school of thought, humans are more susceptible to self-deception because we choose to hold on to certain beliefs. Say for instance, you meet this amazing person who seems to match all of your criteria in dealing with such a person. But underneath that layer, you can sense a withholding or even know outrightly that you are being deceived but rather than act on that instinct, you choose to act on the hope that people can be what they appear to be.

We hear of the expression wolf in sheep clothing all the time. There is no doubt that the wolf may be really good at disguising himself for the sheep just as there is no doubt that the sheep on some primal level were aware of the wolf in their midst but chose to deny the existence of the threat because they wanted to believe that the wolf was one of them. We can all imagine how that story played out. This pattern of behavior over time would dim the alarms bells that resound in our senses whenever a crisis arises because of what we tell ourselves.

Next to denial is rationalization. Denial and rationalization are tools of the same trade. They work handily together in self-deception. Rationalization is essentially how you explain away the situation. I have had female friends (and some of my male friends too in the same boat) who are in a relationship that isn't really healthy for them but rather than end things by taking themselves out of the equation, they somehow always seem to generate more reasons why they should stay put in that relationship. Women in abusive relationships know that a man raising his hand against you is displaying the highest form of disrespect. But I have heard these violent men been described as affectionate and their occasional violence being just one of their ways of showing the woman that they care. This behavior does not only apply to relationships.

People have found themselves working at a place they know exploiting them. But, they tell themselves how jobs are difficult to find and how they would not be able to pay the bills if they leave. And so, they continue to work under those terrible conditions refusing to even protest because they have come to accept the situation as normal thanks to their rationalizations and denials. Whether in our careers or in our normal relationships, a lot of us a leading sad and unfulfilled lives because we have convinced ourselves that we cannot do otherwise, and this is our fate. Some people even go a step further and say they deserve what they are getting because of some misdeed in the past. In other words, they have chosen to open the doors to their own prison cells, lock themselves in and then proceed to act as jailer. Self-deception is a mental prison of some sort but there are merits to it, too.

When confronted with challenges that threaten to overwhelm us, a little bit of self-deception can help to bolster your confidence and even the playing field. You may choose a more positive phrase other than self-deception to describe it, but it doesn't change what it is. People like to call it perp talk, getting psyched or giving yourself a morale boost...whatever you choose to call it, it still boils down to you convincing yourself about something that you are not. A man wanting to approach a very beautiful woman who he feels is out of his league has to convince himself that he is all that. He acts more confident than he actually feels in order to convince himself that he is indeed confident. So, you see, the self-confidence thing can swing both ways. But to avoid falling victim to people who use elements of dark psychology to get their way, you need to recognize the truth for what it is.

If your instincts are kicking in, rather than deny it, ask questions. Find out why you feel the way you do about the person and try to get more answers. When you learn to trust your instincts, you are better able to protect yourself. If a situation is not working out favorably for you, rather than choosing to be powerless about it (because yes, it is choice), you should actively look for a way to escape the situation. Don't lie to yourself. The truth may not be what we want it to be, but you should not have to live out a painful lie just to deny it. Recognize the lies you tell yourself for what they really are.

James W. Williams

IGNORE THE LIS THAT OTHERS TELL US

Lies and secrets…

they are like cancer in the soul

They eat away what is good

And leave only destruction behind.

Cassandra Claire

We are all victims of lies at some point in our lives. That doesn't mean everyone who came into our circle and lied to us was trying to use us to carry out some evil plan of theirs. In fact, there are truths that when told with malicious intent can have the same effect as a terrible lie if not worse. Whether the lies are coming from your best friend, a parent, or even someone from work, the effect can be devastating. In some cases, it is not the lie itself that hurts. It is the knowledge that someone you trusted made the deliberate choice to fabricate a story and convince you that it is real. Certain lies are told by simply not saying anything about it. People think, if I didn't say anything, I didn't lie about it. But in reality, that is called a lie by omission.

It is almost impossible to start with just one lie and leave it at that. One lie leads to another lie that perpetuates another lie until both the person telling the lie and the person being lied to are caught in a tangled web of lies. This web can be so tangled that extricating the truth becomes impossible. Lies have a way of changing you and that change is not always good. This is because you are being fed a fabricated version of reality. Against our better judgement, we buy into these lies and the anger we feel when the truth is unveiled is not entirely directed at the liar in question. We blame ourselves for believing those lies.

When we discover we are being lied to, we often react not just to the person and what they represent, our identity is also being called into question. Your loss of faith is not just in person but in yourself as well. The loss of faith results in doubts. And doubts lead to distrust. But before we get into the effect of lies, let us explore why we fall for the lies in the first place.

I am going to start off with the general populace and then proceed to bring things closer to home. If you have been active online, you will likely notice that the most read and followed stories are the sensational pieces. In recent times, there has been an increase in the pedaling of stories that have no truth to them. Even the prestigious Rolling Magazine which has always been known for their excellent reportorial skills had put up a story (which they believed to be true) that turned out to be false. So, you wonder, how come people with years of skills and experience were able to fall for that kind of lie? If you are expecting some kind of grand revelation of truth, I am sorry to disappoint you. The reason is quite simple and naturally a very human response. They wanted to believe it.

 In the same way, we fall for the lies that people tell us because we want to believe that it is true. This happens on several levels and it is not always linked to people that are very close to us. For instance, if you share a certain political view or opinion, you are more likely to be following or reading articles or posts that support your belief. If someone tells a lie that supports your belief, you are more inclined to fall for that lie because you want it to confirm your own personal beliefs or theories. This also applies in our relationships as well. You believe that love should be a certain way and because a person displays patterns that correspond with what your idea of love is meant to be, you choose to ignore the other tell-tale signs and believe in their lies instead.

Another reason we believe a lie is because we have a personal stake in the lie. A manipulator presents you with an alternative reality that you suspect to be false but because your own personal interest conflicts with the truth, you chose instead to accept the lie. The personal interest may not just be about a personal gain. It could be your special feelings about the person. You like the person, and you have created this halo around that individual. So, you would rather stick to your haloed version of events (self-deception at work here) than face the possible reality that this person may be more sinister than he or she looks and that their ulterior motives may not be for your own best interests at all.

Lies that stem from an altered reality of events are not the only type of lies that can be used to manipulate us. When we think of people lying to us, we are more focused on events that were fabricated for the benefit of the liar, but there are other kinds of lies out there that can be as vicious, if not more, than the altered reality. I am referring to lies that are told to change your perception about yourself. Throughout every chapter in this book, I have strongly emphasized that we are most vulnerable when our emotions come to the forefront, especially when those emotions are spiraling out of control. When a manipulator meets a person who appears to be emotionally stable, he or she knows that it would be difficult to work their devious charms on such a person. So, one's first line of action is to wear down the emotional foundation of that person.

A manipulator looks for chinks in the person's proverbial armor and begin to exploit it. Let's say you are normally a confident person, but you have some insecurities about your body. A master manipulator would key into that concern and twist it by amplifying your fears. It may not come off as a direct insult, but it would be strategically used to imply that the problem is worse than it actually is. Snide remarks about how big you look today to how you need to cut back on the carbs are subtle but effective hints at the problem they are hoping to amplify. When you start accepting these lies, you would find yourself pondering on problems that really aren't issues in the first place. And gradually, the proverbial mole becomes the mountain, and you are promptly buried under insecurities that have eaten away at your confidence until you are exactly what the manipulator wants you to be: a person with poor self-esteem and zero confidence who can be easily manipulated.

If chirping away at your self-esteem does not get the desired results, a manipulator then tries the negative route. Telling you that you cannot do something and using your past experiences and emotions to support this lie until you believe it. Sometimes, the reverse is the case. You are lulled into a state where you feel secure even though the reality is different. This tactic is often used when the perpetrator wants to extract something like money or a favor from you. He or she uses positive reinforcements rooted in lies to give you a false sense of security and then one strikes. It takes mental clarity and effort to see through the lies that people tell in whatever form they appear.

DWELLING ON THE PAST

I have learned that if you must leave a place that you have lived in and loved and where all your yesteryears were buried deep, leave it any way except a slow way, leave it the fastest way you can.

Never turn back and never believe that an hour you remember is a better hour because it is dead.

Past years seem safe ones, vanquished ones, while the future lives in a cloud, formidable from a distance.

Beryl Markham

In a track race, athletes are trained to stay focused and ground themselves in the present. There is no looking back figuratively and literally. Their senses are attuned to the moment. When the race begins, it is all about them, the track, and the finish line. This is because, the second they start paying attention to anything else but the race, they start losing the race. Even in a relay race where the athlete has to look back and take the baton from their running mates, their gaze promptly returns to the track in front of them as soon as the baton exchanges hands. Life is like a race and looking back on the past can distract and hold you back from being the best you can be. And most importantly, this kind of distraction is the type of thing a manipulator would love to use against you.

When the brain is not actively triggering emotions that stems from memories, our mind does a bang-up job of bringing all those emotions to the forefront. I tried to think of how to best explain the firm grip our past can have over us and a scene from one of my favorite movies illustrates this. Without going into the plot of the movie [Pacific Rim], let me set the scene for you. Mako and Raleigh are paired up to try out the Jaeger [a machine designed to destroy the aliens] for the first time and to manipulate the machine, there has to be a mental connection through what they called the mental link. The connection process takes you through a series of memories [your past] before you are rooted in the present. Mako's recollection of her past is so vivid that she becomes trapped in it. This results in her detachment from the present reality. This detachment almost results in her activating a nuclear weapon that could have destroyed the present. Bringing it back to us, our reconnection with our past may not be as vivid, but the psychological threat that dwelling on the past poses is just as potent.

When we talked about emotional scars earlier, we explored the pains/emotions triggered by events and the focus was on our biological defense mechanisms. We know that the brain interprets certain signs from our environment as threats and in so doing, it activates reactions that we are not always able to control. This is somewhat similar to that except this time, we are actively engaging a negative experience by thinking consistently on it. And in that process, we unleash an avalanche of emotions that could put us under.
Psychologists refer to this as ruminating. Just like a goat [or

cow] regurgitates the food it ate hours prior and chews on it, we have a tendency to regurgitate our experiences and dwell on them.

But it is not just the negative past that we cling to sometimes, the past has a lot of positive memories that provide us with comfort. This connection makes it difficult to let go of it. Unfortunately, it is just as easy to become disillusioned with the positive past as it is with a negative past. We all know someone in our life who is fond of using the phrase, "the good old days," and we recognize how heartbreaking it can be to watch them cling to the remnants of the so-called glory days. You may not use that phrase, but your fondness of the past can get you quickly stuck in that memory and set you on a path that destroys your chances in the present. Of course, you may want to argue that if bad memories dredge up bad emotions, then good memories bring up good emotions and that cannot be bad. The truth is, as long as it is disconnecting you from the present reality, it is bad. And this is what dark psychology exploits.

When you live your life in the past, you get yourself rooted in a situation that either slows you down or stop you from moving forward. Fear is one of the most powerful emotions that our memories can activate. And it is not just the famous fear of the boogieman [or whatever inspires serious fear in you] that keeps you down. The fear of uncertainty can also hold you back. You might be holding on to a certain relationship, job or lifestyle simply because you are afraid of what would happen if that thing or person is no longer in your life. And that fear keeps you there even when the situation is not ideal for you.

This is not denial because you are aware of the wrongness of the situation. You have just decided to put your focus on what was and distance yourself or worse, accepted what is because you are afraid of what will/might be. Besides, you should believe that manipulators and saboteurs in your life would capitalize on this fear and work their deviousness to exploit this knowledge until they can get what they want. Their modus operandi would be to somehow strengthen the grip that this past has on you and convince you that the present reality is a necessity. They use your insistence on focusing on the past to discredit your present and rob you of a future. The irony here is that you are at least partially aware of what is happening, but you have made a conscious or subconscious decision remove yourself from the equation, so you justify your decision with an event that has already happened.

In essence, you yourself have created this illusion of the absence of choice and given the reins of your presence to others. This is not to say that looking back is completely wrong. Rear view mirrors were created specifically for this purpose. The point here is, if you really want to separate the truth from the lies, staying rooted in the present is one way to go about it. Psychologists say that people who dwell on the past are more likely to be depressed than others. Depression is one of those dark emotions that leave you vulnerable. And if you do get into treatment for the depression, one of the steps to overcoming it is to retrace your steps in the past, coming to terms with the reality of the situation, and then applying the lessons learned from the revisited past before letting go.

If you have a problem letting go, you only need to remind yourself that you have absolutely no control over what has happened. No matter how much you revisit it and dwell on it, you cannot change what has happened. The same can be said of the future. There are many possibilities. Sure, the steps you take now could to an extent determine what happens tomorrow but there are too many variables to accurately predict the future. What you own and have total control over is what you do right now. Detach yourself from the past and from the fears of the future and put your focus on the "right now."

James W. Williams

BLIND OPTIMISM

I am not interested in blind optimism,
But I am very interested in optimism that is hard won.
That takes on darkness and then says, "that is not enough."

Colum McCann

When we accept responsibilities in life, we do so with gusto and enthusiasm. And as with everything in life, we encounter challenges which could range anywhere from mild obstacles to raging storms that seem to be bent on destruction...our destruction. In those times, your zeal and enthusiasm might wane. What keeps you from giving up and gets you through that rough patch is optimism. But there are different levels to this thing called optimism and not all of them have the same positive impact in our lives. There is a kind of optimism that appears to disconnect you from the reality and that type of optimism is known blind optimism. But before we get into that, let us look at that aspect of human nature that makes us want to believe in an alternate outcome even when we are facing a very dire situation. Just like the author of the quote above, we are interested in what makes us unflinching in the face of darkness.

Like all facets of human emotional behavior, it appears that we are simply hardwired to be optimistic, not just in the face of danger. This behavior is present in our simple everyday activities. You have a product that is maybe a few days past its expiry date, but you go ahead to eat it anyway in the hope that it would not cause any harm to you. Or you are approaching the traffic lights just as it changes colors and rather than slow to a stop, so you speed up in the hope that you would make it past the lights without getting caught. Or maybe you are even taking the chance to ask a person out in the hopes that he or she would feel the same way about you, as opposed to throttling over your exposed feelings on the floor with a sledgehammer? It is part of your emotional reflex. Despite Murphy's Law, you are optimistic because you are human.

However, some people take this optimistic approach in their dealings a tad too far. Instead of just pushing the boundaries as I illustrated with the examples above, they put absolute faith in the possibility that the good outcome they are hoping for would outweigh the likelihood of things going wrong. This kind of thinking inspires a reckless behavior that could have a painful ending if the emotion is not checkmated. Being optimistic delivers many health and mental benefits. If you have ever read the book, *The Power of Positive Thinking* by Norman Vincent, you are no doubt furnished with information on just how well positive thinking can serve you. Medical studies show that people who are optimistic are more than likely to recover from life-threatening sicknesses than people who are the opposite. Overall, optimism can blind you.

Blind optimism is a form of self-deception. In this case, you are not just thinking that you have a good chance of getting the desired positive outcome. You have deluded yourself into thinking that things would play out the way you hoped they would: because they are banking on the positives of the situation, they do not take any steps to protect themselves in the event that things go awry because they are not even entertaining any negative notion. When you are blinded by optimism, you have a higher tendency to rationalize and explain away the reality of the situation. Even when you are presented with the gravity of the situation, your blind optimism keeps you from taking any action that would mitigate negative outcomes.

As I said earlier, we fall for a lie because we want to do so. Blind optimism is a kind of lie that also works in distancing us from the reality of things. You find yourself confronting a lie directly in the face, but perhaps because accepting the reality that this person or situation is not what they seem or appear to be might be too hurtful, we turn on the optimism switch a notch higher. Our need to want to believe that people are not as terrible as they may be makes us give in to demands that have a negative impact on us. In turn, we replace that negative gut instinct with a bright reaction straight out of the pages of the book of blind optimism. And often times, we do this because we want to feel good about the situation or about the person.

Blind optimism affects your ability to accurately assess the pitfalls and problem areas in any given situation. It puts you in a mental state where you are almost walking on clouds and gives you a false sense of security. You feel invincible to the risks and fail to take precautions. The plus side of blind optimism is that you are more likely to take on risks than most. In business, people who are blindly optimistic are usually in the early adopters' category. When a new product hits the market, while others are busy calculating the risks and trying to assess their odds, these guys dive in feet first. Many new business counts on these types of people.

In day to day living, blind optimism creates a dangerous detachment from reality. It is like a person who wakes up in the morning and decides that he wants to skydive. Giving no thought to altitudes, weather conditions or landscape, he just buckles on his parachute and dives. The chances of hitting a rock before deploying one's parachute is just as high as making it to the ground in one piece. But one chooses to prepare for only the reality that one is willing to accept. You cannot deal with people in the same manner and not expect some sort of negative backlash. There is ignorance and then there is the willingness to see the danger ahead and chose to do nothing about it. It doesn't matter if this person is your best friend, your mother, or your partner. If you spot the signs that could imply something else is at work, wishing and hoping that you are wrong is not going to protect you if you are right. Sure, it might temporarily keep that relationship in a good place, but in the long run, even that too would disintegrate. Taking off the blindfold would require you being truthful with yourself.

There is a common saying that the truth is bitter. I wish I could say that this wasn't the case. When it comes to your relationships with people, bitter is an understatement in the description of the truth. Confronting the reality of the situation can birth a pain that you never imagined and for a while, it is going to hurt. In a situation where your emotions are being taken advantage of, you cannot afford to bury your head in the sand because you don't want to face the reality of your experience. Even a gradual revelation is not helpful.

What you need to do is rip off the Band-Aid and face the emotions squarely. The truth hurts, but it will also set you free. You just need to remind yourself that it is all that this pain is all part of the process and the hurting brings you one step closer to healing.

THE VICIOUS CYCLE

Once you believe that things are permanent,

you are trapped in a world without doors.

Genesis P. Orridge

The four walls that imprison us in a web of deceit are the lies we tell ourselves, the lies that others tell us, dwelling on the past and blind optimism. Each of them is a facet of the false realities that entraps us and on their own, they can have a ghastly impact on us, but when you have all the elements working together, the results can be devastating. People who have escaped or lived through lives where they were manipulated incessantly can identify at least 3 of these elements at work when the manipulations were at its peak.

As with all forms of deceptions, it starts out with a lie. The lie is not easily discernable in the beginning. Perhaps, on an instinctive level, you get the sense that something is not right, but there is almost nothing concrete to base your feelings on, so you decide to go with the lie. The decision to go with the lie does not always happen on its own. You don't just accept the lie. On a personal level, you would have to convince yourself to believe the lie and this usually requires you lying to yourself. You remind yourself it is not as bad as it looks. You tell yourself that this person has no reason to lie to you. Basically, you convince yourself anything you need to convince yourself that your instincts are wrong. To help give substance to the lie you are reiterating, you throw in a good measure of unrealistic expectations under the guise of being optimistic. This optimism further impairs your better judgement and leaves you even more vulnerable than you initially were. And to eliminate any doubts, you draw on a past experience to validate your present choices and from there things go downhill. The situation does not always play out like this. Sometimes, one come comes before the other, but the objective is the same: to trap and deceive you.

When this cycle is in play, the manipulator becomes the puppeteer and you become the puppet. The strings with which they use to pull you around would be your emotions. They jerk you around to do their biddings. Now it is important to remember that a person's ability to successfully manipulate another does not make them a diabolical master planner. These events often play out to a natural order of things. When you leave something of value outside your home and a thief comes along and swipes it, you cannot say that he or she plotted the incident. By nature, these people have groomed themselves to be takers. Whether they have the consent of the owner or not, they are inclined to just take especially when it is put out there for them. In the same vein, a manipulator is inclined to turn the emotions of others against him or her to work to one's own personal advantage. Emotions are to a manipulator what a wand is to a magician, and con artists use emotions to their advantage.

There is a broad spectrum of emotions that the average human experiences. And knowing that emotions are the tools that manipulators use to exploit us might make you want to instinctively shut down your emotions. And I can relate with that line of thinking. But the truth is, numbing your emotions could have an adverse negative effect. For starters, numbing your emotions could lead to you trying to find escape in other places like drugs and alcohols, which gives you the illusion of being not feeling when in actuality, it amplifies your feelings. Besides, the choice to numb your emotions [if such a thing was possible] would mean not experiencing the good stuff as well. Because, while you want to purge negative emotions like greed, anger and sadness, you want to experience joy, happiness and peace, too. The emotions are some of the things that make sour existence as human that more valuable and getting rid of these emotions would be akin to living in a world without color. Instead of trying to numb these emotions, we can exert more control over them and use them to help us grow as individuals.

And this brings us to the next important topic. Control. While manipulators work with our emotions against us, their biggest weapon is having us believing that we have no control. This grand illusion has us thinking we are powerless and helpless and there is nothing we can do about it. But if you review this section of the book, heck if you go all the way back to the beginning, you will realize something very interesting. The common denominator in all of this is you and for their plans to work, it requires some form of consent from your part. I am not saying that what has happened or is happening to you is your fault. No, far from it. All I am trying to say is that you are not as helpless as you seem. One of the reasons I wrote the book is to help those who are under the influences of dark psychology to escape and overcome its hold. And the first step to achieving this is embracing the powers you have. Your emotions can make you vulnerable, but with the right application of knowledge, your emotions can equally become your greatest ally in this battle.

You have a choice and you have a voice. Don't let anyone convince you otherwise. In the next chapter, we will examine in depth how to break free from the whole. Right now, I want you to look inward as though you are looking into the mirror. Embrace your emotions: the fear, the rage, the pain. These feelings are all a part of you. It may not paint a perfect picture, but for one moment, put your expectations for perfection on the shelf. Focus instead on what you feel right now. Whether those emotions are good or bad, make a choice to want better for yourself. The sky would not open, there will be no celestial music playing somewhere in the heavens and your situation will not change overnight. On the contrary, things might have to get worse before they get any better. But when you make this choice, you are mentally preparing yourself for what is to come next.

And if you need a more tangible reason to push for this sudden upheaval from what you have come to accept as your comfort zone, remind yourself that you are enough reason for this to happen. You deserve better, your opinions matter and there is no other person who is more powerful and more instrumental in influencing this change that you desire than you. Right up to this moment, you have looked out for others. You tailored your needs to suit the expectations of others, you put aside your sense of self in other to accommodate the needs of others and for long, you have stayed on the back shelf and depreciated in value. But no more. Now is the time to look out for your own interest and there is no shame in that. That negative voice or the manipulator in your life would want to tell that you are being selfish. Counteract this obvious lie with the truth. The truth is that your ability to care and look out for others begins with the choice to look after yourself first. Therefore, you are being "selfish" at the moment is the best step you can take to becoming selfless.

James W. Williams

PART FIVE:
HOW TO BREAK FREE

ACCEPT THAT YOU HAVE A PROBLEM

Often times, it's not about becoming a new person,

but becoming the person you were meant to be,

and already are but don't know how to be.

Heath L. Buckmaster

We often dwell more on the opinion of others and prioritize how the world sees us or how we want the world to see us. The lifestyle trend of this current age has its own slogan, "fake it until you make it." This kind of approach to living causes us to have a fast and loose relationship with reality. We are so caught up in faking it that we are unable to pull off the mask even when we are alone with ourselves. This form of self-deception can ingrain itself so deeply in our lives that we might wake up one day and find ourselves in a situation that greatly contradicts the fake reality we have worked so hard to preserve and sometimes shocks us to our very core. If we are to be entirely honest, we are not always caught off guard by the lies that are told to us. On some level, we know. What makes us off guard is how much we are hurt by it. And it is this hurt that makes us shy away from the problem in the first place. To break free, the first step is confronting the situation and breaking off any illusions. You cannot go any further if you do not shatter the illusions that surround you. Arm yourself with the knowledge that you have a choice. Then make the conscious choice to see things for what it is. That deal that seems too good to be true might actually be just that...too good to be true.

Next, trust your gut instincts. There are times that a lie has been so masterfully fabricated that it appears to be true. But on some instinctive level, you can sense an imbalance between what should be, what is and then what is being projected to you. There may not be any physical signs to show that hey, something is wrong, but you have a sense that something is amiss. In times like that, it is easy to just dismiss those feelings and go with what you are being told. You may not want to appear rude or be perceived in a certain light, so you give in and ignore that inner voice. Learning to trust your instinct requires practice over time. You start by training yourself on small and simple things. Perhaps you are about to leave the house and you get the urge to go back in and check on something. Or maybe, you just thought of someone and felt the need to call him or her. These are tiny instances and may not lead to large payoffs, but it builds your confidence in your instincts, so that when situations of true consequence arise, you are better able to discern what your instincts are telling and act on them. If you are already in a situation and don't have the time to train your ability to trust your instincts, you should not lose hope. Your instincts are there to protect your best interests. And as long as you are alive, you have instincts that want to help you stay alive. In this situation, you just want to get out of it. So, what are your instincts telling you?

That question would lead you to this next step. Ask the right questions. Start with yourself. Try to find out why you feel the way you do. Look at your current situation and find out why you are no longer content with the way you feel. Ask yourself why you feel the way you do and see if you can be more specific about your feelings. I reiterated that emotions make you vulnerable, but they can also act as a guide when you feel lost. When you are not able to satisfactorily provide the answers you seek, look outside yourself. Looking outside yourself does not necessarily mean you should confront the predator although it may eventually get to this. I don't recommend going the direct route immediately as you will give the perpetrator an opportunity to present a defense that may further cloud your judgement and not get you the results you desire. It can also clue the person that you might be on to them. This might activate their own fight or flight response. Instead, look to people within your cycle of trust. Given that you are currently trying to navigate through a situation that involves a breach of trust, it may be difficult to suddenly decide who to trust. If you are really concerned about that, then go to someone who has little or no personal stake in the equation. Someone who is not directly related to you or the person(s) involved might be best. These people are more likely to be honest with you.

When you ask the questions, the next important thing is to listen to the answers. This may sound somewhat incredulous because duh, you are going to be listening to the answers. The reality is that our self-deception can cause us to be selective about the responses we get. We tell ourselves we are listening, but we are only really paying attention to the answers we want to hear instead of the answers we are actually getting. You may have shattered the illusions around you, but there is still a part of you that clings to the comfort that those illusions bring. The pain of confronting the reality of the situation would deter you from hearing the real answers to the questions you have asked. Actual listening requires some sense of detachment, but not from reality this time around. You need to detach yourself from your emotions.

Your detachment from our emotions could lead you to the next step which is processing the new information logically. Acting irrationally can complicate situations more than they already are. Letting all the emotions simmer and spring up to the surface makes your exit strategy that much difficult. The irrational part of you when confronted with the truth may want you to just let everything go to hell. Your anger, which is righteously justified, can spur you into taking steps that help pacify your emotions in the short term. But in the long term, you may come to regret those actions. I am not saying you should deny your emotions; I am suggesting don't act based on those emotions. Deal with the situations first and then your emotions later.

ACT QUICKLY

It's the action, not the fruit of the action that is important.

You have to do the right thing.

It may not be in your power,

may not be in your time that there will be any fruit.

But that doesn't mean you stop doing the right thing.

You may never know what results come from your action.

But if you do nothing, there will be no result.

Mahatma Gandhi

You have confronted the reality of your situation, which is usually the hardest part. However, it doesn't end there. You cannot hope that the situation would just go away on its own. Remember, you have a choice in this. Even your inaction is a deliberate choice you have made and like the great Mahatma Gandhi said, if you do nothing, there will be no results. Breaking free from a web of deceit might be exhilarating at first until you have to deal with the outpouring of emotions in the aftermath. The intensity of the emotions experienced may cause us to want to go into denial. And this is a normal process. In the five stages of grief, the first stage is denial. The more you delay in taking action, the deeper and faster your denial sets in. And when denial sets in, there is a very high probability that you would go back to the vicious cycle that characterized this stage of your life. Avoid this by taking prompt action now. It doesn't have to be anything grand. Something as simple as informing your close friend of the reality of the situation can set in motion a series of events that will eventually set you free.

After making the choice to act, you should know that the fabric of illusion is made of tougher material than glass. While I used the term "shatter your illusion," what actually happens is a gradual separation of facts from fiction. With your emotions in high gear, the illusion might be working its way back into your heart by using fragments of your emotions to mend it. When a liar is caught in a lie, he or she may seek to recruit others to enforce that lie when the liar no longer has a hold over you. A deceptive partner, whom you have recently broken up with, might use the other mutual relationships in your life at this point to influence you into changing your mind. The person used may not even be in the liar's league, but he or she was probably just manipulated. Liars have no problems using friends, family and even a religious leader to get what they want. You have to stand up for the choice you have made and make up your mind to see it through.

When the ploy to manipulate you through other people fails, liars often resort to their old method, which is leeching onto your emotions. In divorce situations, spouses use their partner's emotional concerns for their child to drag them down. Threats like if you leave, you are never going to see the kids again are used. In business dealings, there is usually an implied threat to cut the other person off without any form of payment. This is a last-ditch effort by the manipulator to attempt to control their victim. They know that their cars are no longer effective and feeling threatened by their loss of control, they use power plays like this to attempt to gain the upper hand. Power plays usually involves forms of blackmail ranging from petty stuff to deep secrets that were entrusted to them when the relationship was good. The blackmailer may want to get financial payouts, more leverage in the negotiation deal, and for the more sinister individuals, one just seeks control.

At this point, one's actions may have you in a corner, making you want to lash out and react. I strongly advise against this. You will need both your logic and your instincts if you want to get out of this unscathed. Although, the truth of the situation is that when you discover you have been consistently lied to, you become emotionally scarred so, the question of leaving the situation unscathed becomes mute. However, priority should be given to taking the route that allows you to leave that toxic situation, without further harming yourself. Emotionally, you are all over the place. Rage, anger, hurt and disappointment are just a tip of the iceberg. But you need to think logically. Keep your head above water and be alert.

They say that an animal is more dangerous when it feels cornered. For a human, this sense of imminent fear is worse. When a person has been caught in the web of deceit woven by oneself, he or she tries to do everything to protect himself or herself. At that point in time, one's selfish instincts and protective mechanisms kick into overdrive, so one is willing to do anything to avoid facing the consequences of his or her actions. As with human nature, it is not possible to predict the extent they are willing to go to avoid this. So, rather than wave your agenda to bring them to justice in their face, your priority should be ensuring that you are safe. If it is possible, I would recommend a physical separation, even if it is temporary from the person who you feel is manipulating you. Not only does this help in giving you room to think clearly, it can help weaken the hold that they have over you. Being in the same proximity, especially if they are on their own territory can make you more vulnerable to more manipulations.

A Many liars and manipulators switch on their charms when they have been caught. They would appear deeply remorseful, apologetic and may even go to extreme lengths to try and convince you of their remorse. But don't fall for it as this could be just another act and another ploy to manipulate you into taking less drastic measures that they may not find favorable. If you feel your resolve weakening, get out at the very least. That action alone can make a huge difference.

How to Analyze People, Persuasion, and Dark Psychology

GET HELP FAST

The best way to not feel hopeless is to get up and do something.

Don't wait for good things to happen to you.

If you go out and make some good things happen,

you will fill the world with hope, you will fill yourself with hope.

Barrack Obama

When you find yourself trapped by the manipulations of others, one of the emotions you tend to experience is confusion. This contributes to clouding your rational thinking leaving with a sense of helplessness. At this point, you may even be questioning the reality of what you are facing. If you continue to entertain these doubts, it would lead to denial. You will probably want to conclude that you have gotten the entire situation wrong. Perhaps you misinterpreted certain things and came to the wrong conclusion? This kind of thinking will drive right back to the arms of the manipulator. Resist the urge to give in by getting a second opinion. In a health crisis, people go to another doctor to get a second opinion. This is to eliminate any iota of doubt you may have about the first diagnosis and affirm the best course of treatment for you. In the same way, getting the opinion of another person can help you discern the truth of the situation and what your next steps might be. Just remember, it is better to go to someone who has proven countless times that he or she has your best interest.

Now that you have the confirmation you need, do not try to take on the challenge on your own. The situation may not be something you want anyone else to know about. You may be worried that people would call you gullible for being where you are. The truth is that they probably will. But they are entitled to their own opinions. Don't let the fear of what people might say ruin your chance of creating a better life for yourself. You don't have to prove anything to anyone but yourself. The world can think what they want to think. Right now, your priority is coming out of the situation and surviving it enough to thrive. A lie may be small and petty, but when it is being told to with the goal of doing something that you didn't want to do, it hurts. It makes you question everything about yourself and stirs up this internal battle. You should not fan the flames of this battle by throwing in the opinions of people who have no idea what it would mean to walk in your shoes. If you need the extra bit of help, reach out for it and be willing to accept it. If you can handle the situation yourself, by all means please do. Just be certain that whatever decision you take, the goal is to get you out and not into the good books of other people. You deserve more than that.

When you have the help you need, the next step is to confront the perpetrator. I suggest you pick the scene or location for this. Chose somewhere that you know gives you the upper hand. This would require some careful planning on your part. If the perpetrator exists in the cyber world, you would have to involve the police and relevant authorities, especially if the person swindled you of your money. Do some preliminary investigation of your own. There are software applications that run facial recognition on popular social media sites like Instagram and Facebook. Look for clues to the person's true identity in the conversations you have had and only when you are armed with enough evidence, you should confront him or her. If the confrontation happens before you have evidence, you risk spooking them and sending him or her into one's hideouts. Of course, with the authorities involved, you would still get them eventually, but it could take longer than it normally would if you had patiently prepared yourself before doing the confrontation.

When it is someone who lives in close proximity to you, things may have to be done differently. If you fear for our life in any way, please do not confront this person on your own. In abusive relationships, it is best to avoid confrontations entirely. Simply bid your time and look for the best opportunity to escape. Don't succumb to demands about having "one last conversation". And if you must consent to a meeting like this, please ensure that you are not alone. Notify the people who care about you and have at least one person present during this meeting. Your safety is the priority. If you are in an abusive situation, I strongly advise these precautions:

Reach out to a local organization that caters to victims of abuse in your area. This is probably the best and most important step would take as they have professionals who are there to guide you and counsel you on your next course of action.

Get out while you can. Don't wait for that big pay, the right moment or some significant event. When you get the opportunity, take it and use it. Deal with the aftermath later. And if the opportunity does not present itself, have a safety plan that would lead to your escape. Do all you can to stay alive and as soon as the moment presents itself cease it.

After confronting the perpetrator and taking the necessary steps to leave the situation, you need to commence the healing process promptly. It doesn't matter the scale and gravity to which you were hurt, manipulated, or abused. You need to be able to move past it and waiting for time to "heal" your wounds requires more than sitting on your couch and reliving the past. Time will give you enough distance from your experience, but if you have acquired anything from this book, it is the fact emotional scars almost never heal. If you do not do something about it, an unhealthy scab could form over the wound leaving you just as vulnerable if not more than when you were living the experience. Talk to a counsellor, go to therapy, whatever you chose to do, take an active role in facilitating the healing process. It will not happen overnight, but each day and each step you take in therapy, the closer you will be to getting better.

DON'T COVER UP

It isn't the original scandal that gets people in the most trouble

...it is the attempted cover-up.

Tom Petri

To endure something as trying and traumatic as living with the lies of someone you trust, this trauma can produce a deep psychological effect. When I started this book, my goal was to help people sieve through the lies in their everyday environment and live above the manipulations of others. The entire focus of this book has been 80% on looking inward and the rest on helping you understand what dark psychology really is. But there is one aspect that we did not go into and this is something you are going to have to experience on your own. That aspect is the people who perpetrate these acts. I provided basic information to help you decode elements and traits of dark psychology but that is as far as I can go.

This is because, the people who are most likely to use you and manipulate you are people you have come to love and trust. The duration of the relationship you may have had with them does not guarantee that they are incapable of hurting you. Sometimes, the times spent with you helps cement your trust in them making you more vulnerable and more susceptible to their charms. That is not to say all the relationships you have would lead to some form of manipulation down the line or that strangers suddenly pose a lesser trait. My point is, there is no way to simply determine that this person is going to hurt you. The best you can do is look out for the signs I mentioned and keep an open mind because, you may struggle more with the idea that this person you trusted hurt you this way than the actual thing that was done to you.

In such a situation, your first impulse would be to deny. This denial hurts you more than it helps. Rather than cover up, you should face the embarrassing truth head-on. Recognize the situation for what it is. And try not to let your emotions cloud your ability to make rational decisions. Because yes, being manipulated sucks and people who do it deserve some form of punishment, but we all know that things are usually more complicated than that. What if the person is your sister, brother, spouse, best friend, spiritual leader? How then do you deal with it?

I would start by saying one's status in your life does not automatically make him or her immune to the consequences of one's actions. But there are other factors that might be adversely affected by whatever decision you take. So, the first thing you need to do is face the embarrassing truth that this person failed and hurt you with scheming and actions. Next, decide on if this relationship is worth continuing. Your partner cheating on you and lying about it all this while is terrible, but do you really what it to be the end of that relationship? Are there kids involved? What happens if you suddenly cut your partner off? You need to know that in a situation like this, cutting the person off is not the only answer. So, ask yourself the right questions. I would start off by asking, barring the offence they committed, how was the relationship? Was it good? Is it worth salvaging? Is the person ready to put in the amount of work required to make things right again? Are you ready to put in the work?

If you decided to call it quits, you would need to figure out how to manage the relationships that are linked to the fallout from this. If there are no ties, proceed to the next chapter on forgiving yourself. If there are ties, depending on the nature of the ties, both of you may have to come together with a narrative on how you want to proceed. If those ties are fickle, you can simply choose to go your separate ways without giving anyone any additional information as you owe them no explanation. Do your best to heal and move on without damaging any other relationship unless you have to. If you decide to continue with your relationship with the person, you have your work cut out for you because, it is going to be a hard, long uphill battle. You will get through it no doubt, but not without will and effort.

Both parties would have to show their willingness to heal the relationship. Apologizing profusely is a good start, they would need to do more than that. The fabric of trust has been ripped apart and mending it is going to require time effort and commitment to it. Both of you should be realistic in your expectations of each other. The person who defaulted will have to work hard on regaining your trust. And the person hurt will have to work hard at learning to believe that person again. There will be glitches in this initially, but the renewed commitment to keep at it daily will propel the relationship forward.

For starters, you might want to give each other space after the initial crisis. The space could be anything from a few days to a couple of weeks, but it should not exceed a month. Use this time to process your feelings about the incident. Try to separate the person from their action because as hurtful as their actions were, there are many factors that could have contributed to it. It may seem like making excuses, but it isn't. Circumstances can cause people to take certain actions, but those actions do not entirely define their character. If you have made the decision to mend this relationship, you may have to take this approach in your thinking.

Next, keep the line of communication open. I am not saying that you have to analyze every single thought between the two of you. Just don't shut each other out. Conversations may seem stifled at first, but with time, you guys can back into rhythm. Be honest in your conversations but try not to speak out of spite. Avoid bringing up the past every time you have an argument. Clinging to what has happened makes it difficult to go past it and grow to where you want to be. Stay rooted in the present. Remember, living in the past has no real benefit.

Above all, trust that you have made the right decision. When you discover that you have been manipulated and lied to, it is not just trust in others that is broken. It is trust in yourself as well. You question your judgement at every turn. Stay rooted in the present and trust that you have made the right and rational decision to mend things. But don't heighten the pressure on yourself by making it mandatory that the new relationship must work. Put in the effort, put in the time. But don't feel disappointed if things don't work out the way you were expecting.

FORGIVE YOURSELF

Take a walk through the garden of forgiveness

and pick a flower of forgiveness for everything you have ever done.

When you get to that time that is now,

make a full and total forgiveness of your entire life

and smile at the bouquet in your hands because it truly is beautiful.

Stephen Richards

People assume that when you have been wronged, the main party that requires forgiveness is the person that committed the offense in the first place. Usually, they are right. But in a situation like this one, where a relationship was established with the offender and that offender took advantage of the relationship, one of the unlikely people who require forgiveness is the victim. There is a reason why even when ties have been severed with the offender, you still find yourself experiencing emotions like depression, anger, irritability, anxiety, and mood swings among other things. These are normal emotions to experience, but you may not be experiencing them for the reasons you think. There is a very strong possibility that the reason for all of these emotions is guilt and shame. This guilt does not stem from something you think you did wrong. It is rooted in the thinking that you did something you were not supposed to do.

You feel guilty for being gullible, vulnerable and for generally putting yourself in a situation where you were easily manipulated in the first place. You are feeling guilty about the hurt you think you brought on yourself. We have all been in this situation at some point. We feel guilty that either our actions or inactions led to the hurt of others even though we were not directly involved in the perpetration of the act. The first thing you need to do is remind yourself that regardless of what happened, it is not your fault. You may not be able to change this perception overnight, but over time by constantly reminding yourself of this fact, you will start believing yourself. To further affirm this belief, you should also remind yourself that the lessons you have obtained from this has put you in a better position to protect yourself against any similar incident from occurring in the future.

The next thing is to accept that the past is not something you can change. It has happened, you have learned, and you have moved on. There is no need to keep reliving the experiences you had. Dwelling on the what ifs, what might have been, what you could have, should have and would have done cannot in any way change a single second of what has already happened. The best you can do is pick up the lessons you have learned and shape them into the new principles to live by. You have bravely accepted the reality of the situation despite the lies you were told. Now is the time to accept that this business was concluded in the past and it stays there. You may be dealing with the aftermath of the crisis, but that doesn't mean that it is still happening. Take each day as it comes and finds more reasons to look forward instead of looking backward. If you are feeling so anxious about the past, you can take out a day to re-enact the past. One way to do this is by having a mental re-do. Write down what you think you could have done to change things giving all that you do know now. And then move on from it. The purpose of this exercise is to give you some sort of control over what has happened. Take back your power and move on to the next thing.

Now that you have re-written the past, it is time for you to turn over the next page and begin the next chapter of your life. Start by tackling your regrets. These have a way of compounding our feelings. Accept that you did the best you could do under the circumstances and give yourself room to grow. Remember, yours was not a crime. You just had the misfortune of trusting the wrong person. Assign the blame to the right person. Using affirmatives like "I always fall for the wrong person" or "I am so gullible" is very self-limiting. Dig deeper into yourself to find out exactly where those thoughts are coming from. It is only when you have identified the underlying emotion that you can move past these negative affirmations. And the longer you accede to these negative phrases, the more acute your anxiety levels are going to get. This is because you might become somewhat paranoid about your relationships with people, seeing enemies only were friends and reading the wrong meaning in every action.

Finally, there is the issue of love. We may be harsh in our dealings with others but the person we are most harsh with is ourselves. We find it easier to forgive the perpetrator than to forgive ourselves and the cost of this behavior is self-destructive patterns that are evident in our other relationships. We sabotage those relationships before they even begin. Using the guise of preventing another manipulative relationship, we destroy new relationships. The real reason for this behavior is the loss of the feeling of self-love. Deep down inside, you don't feel you deserve love but because you would rather hear that from yourself, you burn bridges. There are pills to help you cope with the anxiety and depression, but there are no pills to get to that place where you fall completely in love with yourself. That would require some work and at the end of the day it is worth it. There are no hard or fast rules on how to begin this journey to self-discovery. However, I believe that waking yourself up daily with positive affirmations like, "I love myself and I deserve to be loved" is a start. It's cheesy at first, but highly effective in the long run.

And when you have resolved your issues with the past, forgiven yourself and begun the process of learning to love yourself, it is now time to let go. All that pain, all that negativity, all that anger…own it for a moment and then let go. All the steps listed in this chapter are great, but the healing process is only completed when you let go.

TRUST YOUR INSTINCTS

Trust your hunches.

They are usually based on facts filed away just below the conscious level.

Dr. Joyce Brothers

In one of the earlier chapters, we touched on this briefly. I decided to dedicate a whole chapter to this because when you are dealing with the forces of dark psychology, your primary defense against it is your instinct. While your brain is interpreting signals based on facts, logic and sometimes experience, your heart is working on the opposite end, sieving information through a filter of emotions. Your gut instinct is the only thing picking up vibrations that neither the heart nor the brain can explicate. And if you can groom yourself to that point where you recognize your inner voice and are trained to react to it, you reduce your chances of being seduced by people trying to work their manipulative will on you.

For starters, recognizing this voice is hard. And that is because over the course of our lives, we have allowed voices of doubt, self-discrimination as well as the loud voices of the critics within and without to drown out our authentic voice. This voice or instinct is hinged on your survival. So, trust that when it kicks in, it senses things in your immediate vicinity that your brain neurons can yet process. Some people call it intuition, and some refer to it as instinct, they are undoubtedly the same thing especially when it comes to relationships. To begin trusting your instincts, you have to accept that it may not always make logical sense. If you have ever been in the middle of doing something and suddenly experienced the sensation of being watched, then you know what I am suggesting. You have no eyes at the back of your head, there is no one else in the room with you but you get the tiny shiver that runs down your spine and a "sudden knowledge" that you are being watched. That is exactly what I am talking about.

The first step to connecting with your instinct is decluttering your mind of the voices that you have let in. You can do this with meditation. Forget the "he said, she said" chatter. Focus on your center. That voice that you know is you. Next, pay attention to your thoughts. Don't just dismiss those eclectic monologues you have in your head. Instead go with the flow of the thoughts. Why do you think a certain way about a certain person? How come you feel so deeply about this person even though you have only known each other for a couple of days? What is this nagging feeling you have about this other person? As you explore your thoughts, you become more attuned with your intuition and understand when your instincts kick and how to react to it. If you are the kind of person who prefers to make spur of the moment decisions, you may need to learn to take a step back to pause and think. This moment where you pause gives you a chance to really reflect on and evaluate your decisions.

The next part is a hard part and not many people would be able to follow through on it. Unfortunately, this is not a step you can skip or navigate around. This part involves trust. To be able to trust your instinct, you have to be open to the idea of trusting yourself and trusting others. Your inability to trust others would just make you paranoid and when you are paranoid, it is not your instincts that kick. It is your fear. Fear has the tendency of turning every molehill into a mountain. You have to let go of your fear, embrace trust and let that lead in your new relationships. Without the roadblocks put up by fear in your mind, you are better able to hear the voice within.

Finally, you need to re-evaluate your priorities. If money and material possessions are at the forefront of your mind, you may not be able to see past them. Every interaction you have with people would be interpreted as people trying to take advantage of you and if you dwell on this often enough, it soon becomes your reality. You know how you attract what you think of into your life. If you are constantly thinking about material wealth, you will only attract people who think the same way as you.

Using this as a guide, view all of your relationships; the old, the new and the perspective with this new hindsight. Don't go into a relationship expecting to be played. Whether it is a business relationship, a romantic relationship or even the regular acquaintance, be open when you approach them. That way, you can get the right feedback from your intuition about them. Also, don't step into this thinking that your gut is going to tell you to run in the opposite direction when you meet people who are suspect. It would be a small simple nudge.

I remember an experience I had during one of my travels. I got into this cab. There was nothing physically that I can point out to say this triggered me. I just know that I had this sudden revulsion for the driver. I was overwhelmed by this smell of sweaty armpits. I am not very big on body odors, but I have been caught in situations where I just had to grin and bear it [elevator rides anyone?]. But in this case, I just wanted to get out of his cab. As soon as we pulled into a prominent well-lit spot, I asked to exit, even though it wasn't my stop. Just as I came down, a squad car pulls up next to him. Apparently, the authorities had been notified of its involvement in the robbery and kidnap case. I don't know if he had the same plans for me. All I knew was that the moment I entered; I could not get out fast enough. My instinct did not tell me to run or that hey, your driver is a kidnapper. It just made me feel like there was something wrong about being in the car. It was that simple.

In the same way, your instincts speak to you using a language you understand. Whether it is chills down your spine, goosebumps or just a sudden need to puke, you will recognize that feeling when you experience it and with practice, you will learn to trust it.

EMPLOY THE BEST PRACTICES IN ALL YOUR DEALINGS

Good, better, best.

Never let it rest.

Until your good is better and your better best.

St. Jerome

Christians have a saying, "you reap what you sow, "which is more than just a biblical phrase. It encapsulates the natural order of things. Of course, we know that bad things sometimes happen to very good people and vice versa. But, never believe for one moment that people do not get their retribution. Because they do. When you have been treated badly in life, you naturally want to shut yourself in and close yourself off to people. And if you have to deal with people, you want to always position yourself where you would have the upper hand. The problem with this kind of thinking is that because of your experiences, you become a victim who has made the decision [at least on a subconscious level] to make other people victims.

You may be able to find temporary pleasure in dealing the same card that other people have dealt you to innocent people but the damage in the long run can be devastating. Plus, you could end up setting off a chain of events with a domino effect that could come back to you. Even when you are presented with the opportunity, don't take it. Instead, turn the situation around by choosing to end the pain cycle with you. As someone who has been here, I can tell you that it is not easy. As a teenager, I was painfully shy. I found it difficult to talk to people. Even when I was with people like my parents and sibling, I still didn't crawl out of my shell entirely. But all that changed when I met Debbie. She was my high school dream, and I remember being painfully in love with her.

It took a lot of mental energy to finally work up the courage to ask her out on a date. And when I did, I was even more blown away by the fact that she said yes. I was walking on sunshine for the next 3 months until I found out that I was just a bet. Yes, I know it sounds remarkably like that teen movie that was a hit back in the day except this time, I was the victim. It hurt more than words can say, but that was not the worst part. I was humiliated the worst way a person like me can be. You know that dream we all have where you are standing on stage in front of the whole school and you suddenly find yourself naked? This was way worse than that.

I am not sure how I was able to get through that month in school much less the entire school year, but I did. Fast forward to my post-college years, I met Debbie again. Let us just say I was in a more advantageous position and I had the option of using my office to make her life difficult, but I chose not to. Initially, she interpreted this to mean I still had feelings for her, and she tried to work that to her advantage. I politely informed her that I was just doing my job. If I had held on to the feelings that I had for her in the past, I would have reacted differently. It was either she would have been successful in her attempts to seduce me or I would have been seduced into using the powers that my position offered to "punish" her. But I did neither. And in that decision, I found true freedom.

Life has a funny way of working itself out smoothly. Don't take it on yourself to be the dispenser of justice. Instead, arm yourself with the lessons learned, and use them to your advantage. Like St, Jerome said in the introductory quote, be your very best...even when you are put to the test.

CONCLUSION

I have heard people caution, "the heart of man is desperately wicked." I don't know who said it or where I heard it, but it stuck in my head, and I find it to be true. There are no devices or software applications that one can use to decipher the thoughts of another person. The best you can do is understand your own thoughts and feelings and do your best to live out your principles and values. But just because you can't tell if your new best friend is betraying or not should not mean you should spend your days obsessing over it.

Because yes, the true intentions of a man's heart are hidden. However, man's capacity to do good is equally as great as it is to go the other way, and this is not the best part. The best part is that for every single person who has hurt you in the past, there are a hundred more who want to do good by you. It may sound incredulous, but this is the reality of the situation. This book was not written to scare you into retreating into your shell and avoid dealing with people. On the contrary, I wrote it to help you make better choices in your relationships.

By understanding the tricks and tools that certain employ in their dealings with others, you are better equipped to protect yourself from such vices. And if you have been hurt by people, this book is meant to help you with the healing process. Nothing in life is ever concluded. We may have come to the end of the book, but it doesn't mean that your process has ended. If you take the lessons that I have shared with you to heart, you can successfully open yourself to the wonderful prospects life has in store for you. The journey to attaining a deeper understanding of self and discovering yourself on its own is a highly rewarding experience.

So, close this book, but keep your heart and mind open. Some of the clichés in life have a tremendous impact on our lives. Love hard, smile more, and most importantly, let go. Life is too precious and too wonderful to live it any other way. And always wake yourself up with the reminder that you deserve the best that life has to offer. Thank you for taking me on this journey with you!

Thank you

Before you go, I just wanted to say thank you for purchasing my book.

You could have picked from dozens of other books on the same topic but you took a chance and chose this one.

So, a HUGE thanks to you for getting this book and for reading all the way to the end.

Now I wanted to ask you for a small favor. **Could you please consider posting a review on the platform? Reviews are one of the easiest ways to support the work of independent authors.**

This feedback will help me continue to write the type of books that will help you get the results you want. So if you enjoyed it, please let me know.

Lastly, don't forget to grab a copy of your Free Bonus book *"Bulletproof Confidence Checklist"*. If you want to learn how to overcome shyness and social anxiety and become more confident then this book is for you.

Just go to: https://theartofmastery.com/confidence/

www.ingramcontent.com/pod-product-compliance
Lightning Source LLC
LaVergne TN
LVHW051915060526
838200LV00004B/163